TOWARDS ANOTHER
ARCHITECTURE

TOWARDS ANOTHER
ARCHITECTURE

NEW VISIONS FOR THE 21ST CENTURY

EDITED BY OWEN HOPKINS

Farrell
Centre

First published in 2024 by Lund Humphries

Lund Humphries
Huckletree Shoreditch
Alphabeta Building
18 Finsbury Square
London EC2A 1AH
UK

Newcastle University   School of Architecture Planning & Landscape

www.lundhumphries.com

Towards Another Architecture: New Visions for the 21st Century
© Owen Hopkins, 2024
All rights reserved

ISBN: 978–1–84822–677–7

Cover image: Begun in 2010 by Andrew Kovacs, 'Archive of Affinities is a constantly updated collection of architectural images . . .'
https://o-k-o-k.net/ARCHIVE-OF-AFFINITIES
Credit: Andrew Kovacs

Copy edited by Pamela Bertram
Designed by Jacqui Cornish
Proofread by Patrick Cole
Cover design by Paul Arnot
Set in Mundial
Printed in Estonia

CONTENTS

Contributors   7
Foreword by Sir Terry Farrell   11

Introduction: Architecture *and* Revolution   13
Owen Hopkins

KNOWLEDGES

1   Learning from the Vernacular in Senegal: The Architecture
of Worofila   41
Nzinga Biegueng Mboup

2   One Step Back, Two Steps Forward: Pluralism, Post-Modernism
and Architecture in the Climate Emergency   53
Dávid Smiló

3   From Cautionary Tales to Stories of Active Hope: The More-
Than-Human Work of Superflux   63
Anab Jain and Jon Ardern

SITES

4   Atemporal Wisdoms: Re-Learning Architecture in the
Rural Context   77
Xu Tiantian

5   Towards a Liquid Architecture   87
Gonzalo Herrero Delicado

6   Another Way of Writing: Reimagining Architecture Criticism   97
Marianela D'Aprile

ALLIANCES

7   The Adaptive Expertise of the Collaborating Architect   105
     Ruth Morrow

8   Build Longer Tables, Not Higher Walls: Action, Activism and
     Equality in the Built Environment   113
     Alice Brownfield

9   FIELD: Bio-arts as Platform for Collaboration   123
     *Xenia Adjoubei, in collaboration with Supermrin
     and Jessica Fertonani Cooke*

RESETS

10   Architecture: Abolished or Abolitionist?   139
      V. Mitch McEwen

11   Home Revolution: Equality Beyond Representation
      in the Work of Edit   151
      Marianna Janowicz

12   Towards a Queer Architectural History   159
      Joshua Mardell
      Untoward Architecture   162
      Adam Nathaniel Furman

Notes   167
Bibliography   171
Index   173
Acknowledgements   176

CONTRIBUTORS

Xenia Adjoubei is an urban designer and researcher in emergent technology, sustainability and spatial experience and leads the FIELD bio-arts project at Inclusive Ecologies Incubator, Pratt Institute, New York, where she is Visiting Assistant Professor. She specialises in areas of culture, cities and post-automation futures, and is Lead Researcher in the Global Free Unit, a network for education through live projects in contexts of rapid economic and political change. Prior to moving to New York, Xenia ran Adjoubei Scott-Whitby Studio, an architecture and urban design practice specialising in public realm, climate justice and territorial modelling.

Jon Ardern is an artist, designer, technologist and co-founder of Superflux, a critically acclaimed foresight, design and technology company in London working for clients such as the V&A, Google, UNDP and the BBC. His work has won honours from UNESCO, Innovate UK, the European Commission and New York's Social Design Network. His work has been exhibited at MoMA New York, CCCB Barcelona, the National Museum of China, Vitra Design Museum and V&A London, and has been featured in *WIRED*, *Business Insider*, *Dezeen*, *The Guardian* and the *Evening Standard*, amongst others. Jon led Superflux's most ambitious projects such as Mitigation of Shock and Drone Aviary. His work can be found at www.superflux.in. You can follow him on X/Twitter @jonardern.

Alice Brownfield is an architect, co-chair of Part W (an action group campaigning for gender equity in the built environment) and trustee for Action on Empty Homes. She is also a Director at Peter Barber Architects – a London-based practice renowned for a number of groundbreaking urban social housing and homelessness projects (and winner of the 2021 RIBA Neave Brown Award for Housing). Alice is the recipient of the 2021 MJ Long Prize for Excellence in Practice in recognition of her housing work and advocacy for equity in the built environment, and has been a design tutor, visiting critic and lecturer at a number of UK schools of architecture.

Marianela D'Aprile is a writer and the deputy editor of the *New York Review of Architecture*. Her work on politics, art, architecture and culture has been published widely, including in *The Nation*, *Jacobin*, *Artnet News* and *The Avery Review*.

Gonzalo Herrero Delicado is a London-based curator, educator and architect working at the intersection of design, art and technology, exploring their connection to ecology and digital culture. He is the Director of The Otherr Agency and an Associate Lecturer at Central Saint Martins and the Royal College of Art in London. Previously, he was the Director of the Ecocity World Summit 2023 at the Barbican Centre, London, and from 2016 to 2021, he was the Curator of the Architecture Programme at the Royal Academy of Arts. His curatorial portfolio includes projects for the Museum of the Future, V&A, Design Museum, Mies van der Rohe Foundation and The Architecture Foundation.

Adam Nathaniel Furman is an artist and designer based in London. Trained in architecture, Adam's atelier works in spatial design and art of all scales, from video and prints to large public artworks, architecturally integrated ornament, as well as products, furniture, interiors, publishing and academia.

Owen Hopkins is a writer and curator. He is Director of the Farrell Centre at Newcastle University which he has led since late 2019, building towards its public opening in April 2023. He was previously Senior Curator at Sir John Soane's Museum, and before that, Architecture Programme Curator at the Royal Academy of Arts. He is the author and editor of numerous books and journals, and writes regularly for the architectural press and beyond. He is the curator of a range of exhibitions, projects and events series – including the one held across 2021 and 2022 from which the present book derived. A frequent commentator on architecture in the press, on radio and TV, he lectures internationally and is a regular guest critic at architecture schools, as well as a judge for a number of architecture awards.

Anab Jain is a filmmaker, designer and futurist. She is the co-founder of Superflux, a pioneering speculative design and experiential futures company in London, UK, working for clients and commissioners such as V&A, Google, the Red Cross, UNDP, IKEA, Deepmind and many more. Anab has delivered prolific talks at TED, Skoll, NEXT, the House of Lords and the House of Commons, UK, and shown work at MoMA New York, V&A London, the National Museum of China and the Museum of the Future Dubai. Profiles on Anab and Superflux can be found in the *Wall Street Journal*, *Business Insider* and the *Financial Times*. Anab is also a Professor for Design Investigations at the University of Applied Arts, Vienna. Her work can be found at www.superflux.in.

Marianna Janowicz is an architect, writer, educator and member of the feminist design collective, Edit. Her research investigates sites and infrastructures for reproductive labour in the home and in the city. Her work has been exhibited at the Oslo Architecture Triennale and MAXXI in Rome, and her writing has been published in the *Architectural Review*, *e-flux Architecture* and the *New York Review of Architecture*, among others. In 2022/2023 Marianna was a Design Researcher in Residence at the Design Museum in London. She teaches at the University for the Creative Arts and the London School of Architecture.

Joshua Mardell is an architectural historian. He is a Tutor (Research) at the Royal College of Art, London, and Co-Editor of the *Journal of Architecture*.

Nzinga Biegueng Mboup is a Dakar-based, Senegalese architect who co-founded Worofila, a practice that specialises in bioclimatic architecture and construction using earth and biomaterials sourced locally. In addition to her architectural practice, Nzinga has worked as a researcher for the African Futures Institute and co-authored two research projects, Habiter Dakar and Dakarmorphose, that investigate the problematics of housing, heritage and identity in the city of Dakar. Nzinga has also co-produced the installation Bunt BAN as a participant in Guests from the Future at the 2023 Venice Architecture Biennale, and starting in the summer 2023, she has been appointed as the curator of the c/o Dakar programme of the Canadian Centre for Architecture.

V. Mitch McEwen is an Assistant Professor at Princeton University School of Architecture, teaching design studios, seminars on urbanism and technology, and building systems. She is principal of Harlem-based design practice Atelier Office, director of architecture and technology research group Princeton Black Box, and co-founder of the Black Reconstruction Collective.

Ruth Morrow is Professor of Biological Architecture at Newcastle University. Ruth's research is largely practice-based and encompasses the material, the social and the ecological. It is driven by an inclusive, feminist ethos and uses tactics of creativity, collaboration and reflection through writing. She has extensive experience in developing material ideas from concept through to commercialisation, resulting in international funding, design awards, exhibitions, chapters, papers, books and citations. She co-leads the research theme, Responsible Interactions, in the Hub for Biotechnology in the Built Environment, and is also head of the new interdisciplinary School X, both based at Newcastle University.

Dávid Smiló is an architect and – together with Attila Róbert Csóka and Szabolcs Molnár – co-founder of Paradigma Ariadné, a Budapest-based design studio established to create architecture and related contents through applying theory, imagination and narration-based design processes. Clients of Paradigma Ariadné include institutions, companies, local governments and individuals, providing them with outstanding ideas and solutions wherever processes require architecture-related knowledge. Paradigma Ariadné took part in several exhibitions and events to display their works in Budapest, Paris, Venice, Warsaw, Vienna, Logroño, Graz and Ohio, USA. Paradigma Ariadné was co-curator with Dániel Kovács of the Hungarian Pavilion at the Venice Biennale of Architecture 2021.

Xu Tiantian is the Founding Principal of DnA_ Design and Architecture and Professor in Practice at Tsinghua University. Born in Fujian in 1975, she received her Baccalaureate in Architecture from Tsinghua University in Beijing, and her Master of Architecture in Urban Design (MAUD) from Harvard Graduate School of Design. Xu Tiantian has engaged extensively in the rural revitalising process in China. Her groundbreaking 'Architectural Acupuncture' is a holistic approach to the social and economic revitalisation of rural China and has been selected by UN Habitat as the case study of Inspiring Practice on Urban-Rural Linkages. She has received numerous awards including the 2022 Swiss Architectural Award, the Global Award for Sustainable Architecture 2023 and the Berlin Art Prize/Kunstpreis Berlin – Architecture 2023. In 2020, she was appointed an Honorary Fellow of the American Institute of Architects.

FOREWORD

It is now a century since Le Corbusier published *Vers une architecture* – a text that has proved influential in shaping the outlooks of generations of architects and urban designers, including myself. While Le Corbusier's buildings remain an exemplar, his ideas – especially those targeted at cities – have not fared as well. As the winds of architectural change blew during the 1970s, I, along with a number of others, felt increasingly constrained by modernist orthodoxy and devoted much energy to developing possibilities for architecture and city-making beyond the principles that Le Corbusier and his followers had laid down so polemically. What later became known as postmodernism emerged, in my work at least, as a means of re-connecting architecture with the city as it existed and the public it aimed to serve.

Today, amid ever deepening climate crisis, transformative digital technologies, and political and economic uncertainty, it is another critical moment for architecture – and for humanity. It is fitting, therefore, that a book as ambitious as *Towards Another Architecture* is the Farrell Centre's first publication, in collaboration with Lund Humphries, bringing together a range of contributors to explore how we might make sense of and develop new ways of working in response to these seismic challenges. Reflecting the centre's ethos in offering a platform of debate and discussion, the book does not privilege any single agenda. Instead, it aims to foster a plurality of transformative ideas, perspectives and outlooks through which a built environment – and a world – that is more inclusive, sustainable and democratic may ultimately emerge.

Sir Terry Farrell

0.1   ARM Architecture's 2001 building for the Australian Institute of Aboriginal and Torres Strait Islander Studies in Canberra, ACT was conceived as a 'black Villa Savoye … an understanding of a local version – an inversion, a reflection of Aboriginal architecture, culture or perceived attitudes'. https://armarchitecture. com.au/projects/australian-institute-of-aboriginal-and-torres-strait-islander-studies/.

INTRODUCTION

ARCHITECTURE *AND* REVOLUTION

Owen Hopkins

> *A great epoch has begun.*
> *There exists a new spirit.*
> *There exists a mass of work conceived in the new spirit;*
> *it is to be met with particularly in industrial production.*
> *Architecture is stifled by custom.*
> *The "styles" are a lie.*
> *Style is a unity of principle animating all the work of an*
> *epoch, the result of a state of mind which has its own special*
> *character.*
> *Our own epoch is determining, day by day, its own style.*
> *Our eyes, unhappily, are unable yet to discern it.*

Le Corbusier, *Vers une architecture* (1923)[1]

Reading these words now over a hundred years since they were written, it is hard, even if one disagrees with them entirely, not to be carried away just a bit by the urgency and clarity of their rhetoric. With the benefit of hindsight, one can readily see why they set the tone for architecture over the following 50 years and why their impact is still being felt – for better and for worse – today.

Le Corbusier's *Vers une architecture* reads as the series of essays from which it originated, published over the preceding years on the pages of the journal *L'Esprit Nouveau* which he had co-founded with the artist Amédée Ozenfant, in 1920. At root, Le Corbusier's argument was an Hegelian one, that architecture should reflect the zeitgeist, the new spirit of modernity. The industrial age necessitated a new style of architecture that would take advantage of its technical innovations and at the same time, in its planning and form, reflect the spirit of the new epoch (to use Le Corbusier's word).

But modernism was not a style, even if that was the terminology Corbusier used. It was a mission: a set of architectural principles – part philosophical, part practical – conceived to be applied anywhere and to any situation. Although it claimed to sweep away all before it, modernism was, on one level, the logical progression of the Enlightenment project of seeking to understand the world through reason and rationality. But where Enlightenment thinkers dealt with the world as it was, modernists aimed to remake it.

That Le Corbusier succeeded in setting the architectural agenda (and of putting himself at the centre of it) was due in no small way to his formidable talent for publicity and self-promotion, the rhetorical force of his polemic, and later built work. But his success also rested – perhaps pivotally – on the fact there was an audience willing to listen and adhere to what he had to say.

Vers une architecture culminated with the famous provocation: 'It is a question of building which is at the root of the social unrest of today: architecture or revolution.'[2] And it's here that the often noted paradoxical conservatism at the heart of Le Corbusier's seemingly progressive mission becomes apparent, because, for him, the answer was clearly the former. Modern architecture, he somewhat self-servingly argued, was the means by which the social, political and economic transformations that industrialisation had unleashed could be mitigated before they spilled over into social and political revolution. In other words, a revolution in architecture was the way in which a broader societal 'revolution can be avoided', as he concluded.[3]

Over following decades, this turned out to be both modernism's greatest strength but also its biggest weakness. Architecture did transform itself – and then the world. Mass housing estates, new schools, new universities, new hospitals, new places of work and production, new civic buildings, new urban infrastructure – modern architecture has been one of the most transformative forces in human history.

Yet while it has indisputably been a force for good, it has also perpetuated power imbalances, discrimination and violence at odds with its apparently emancipatory mission, both locally and globally. This was not simply a noble cause or mission leading to unintended consequences, but the conceptual basis of the mission itself: the contention that its philosophies and prescriptions were universal. As things panned out, architecture was not just a decoy, but also part of the problem.

With a hundred years of hindsight, one of the great ironies of Le Corbusier's messianic vision is that the very thing he so celebrated – unbridled industry – has

0.2 Conceived by Le Corbusier in 1943 and then applied to his buildings beginning with the Unilé d'Habitation in 1952, the Modulor Man is an attempt to (somehow) unite human form, scientific rationality and natural proportion in a single figure, remaking Leonardo da Vinci's *Vitruvian Man* for the modernist age.

led us to our present predicament. Industry and technological progress have undoubtedly delivered transformative changes to living standards, and no one is sensibly suggesting any kind of reversion to pre-industrial ways of living. But the transformations that industry has enabled have come at great cost: global heating, declining biodiversity and pervasive pollution. We are now belatedly coming to the realisation that a world built on fossil fuels is unsustainable on every level.

While the climate emergency is by definition a global phenomenon, its effects are felt locally. The western world remains responsible for the majority of the world's carbon emissions, yet it is the developing world and Global South, which have benefited least from industry, where the effects of climate change will be – and already are – felt the hardest. Such geopolitical imbalances – the legacies of colonisation – mirror social and racial injustices in the western countries that were very often the colonising forces. It is doubly ironic, then, that modernism's universalising mission did not erase difference, but arguably helped entrench it.

Having hurtled along one trajectory for the last 100 years or so, the world has arrived at a crossroads, with the path we choose now determining the next century – and maybe much further still. The levers – architectural or otherwise – we pulled in the past in moments of crisis no longer work and in fact make things worse. If architecture – in its modernist form and since – has played a significant role in leading us to the present predicament, then to help us find a way out, it must change fundamentally, just as it did a hundred years ago. The question this book aims, if not to answer, at least to point a direction towards, is not how architecture has to change, but to what.

* * *

Looking back, it is clear that one of Le Corbusier's critical mistakes – and the one that fatally undermined what came after – was to stifle and smother the raging battle of styles that characterised modernism's earliest incarnations into one, single, monolithic narrative. Then as now, the seismic challenges we face can only be tackled from multiple angles, in multiple dimensions and via multiple perspectives. What we need, therefore, is not a new architecture, as Le Corbusier was popularly mistranslated as advocating, but another one: an architecture that is not bound to a single vision or future, but is diverse, pluralist and sustains multiple conversations about the active role that architects might play in the world.

Encompassing a plurality of ideas, positions and perspectives means fundamentally re-conceiving architecture, not as a new monolithic discipline

0.3   An aerial shot of the *Exposition internationale des arts décoratifs et industriels modernes*, 1925, an exhibition organised to showcase contemporary design across the world. Indicative of its eclecticism, the exhibition would later give its name to the 'Art Deco' style while also featuring Le Corbusier's decidedly modernist Pavillon de l'Esprit Nouveau.

(let alone profession), but as heterogeneous, multivalent, both strategic and tactical, a way of thinking as well as practising that moves through and connects multiple times and realities. We need to expand our definition of architecture, reaching not just beyond buildings, but beyond its seemingly elemental role as shelter, and thinking of it instead as a convenor, a meeting place, a platform for ideas, for people and, ultimately, for the world.

To that end, this book brings together propositions that as a whole begin to articulate what 'another architecture' might mean.[4] They reflect a range of practices and perspectives, techniques and processes, collaborations and geographies, fields and outlooks, and stand in themselves as propositions for different directions and approaches, but also as sparks and provocations for others.

All the contributions exist on the edges of contemporary architectural thinking and practice – just as Le Corbusier's position did a century ago. The question is how to centre them, not in a way that aims for individual hegemony, but in establishing a culture that supports, amplifies and sets in motion possibilities for an ever more heterogenous and polyphonous architecture. This introduction offers some thoughts towards an answer. It looks both back and forwards to consider, via several case studies and scenarios, the macro (and sometimes micro) ways that architectural ideas achieve prominence, the cycles they go through and how disciplinary reinvention can be enacted in ways that are both polemical and inclusive.

*[Architecture] is a western construct, predominantly used within
imperial and colonial processes ... it responds to the rhetoric of
modernity as bringing salvation through civilisation, progress,
development and growth. Architecture operates within the colonial
and imperial logics of extraction of resources, expansion, and the
dispossession of peoples and lands. Put bluntly, it is the rhetoric that
consistently and continuously, in an unbroken colonial continuum,
explains violence, oppression and inequality as 'necessary' or as
'natural' in bringing a modern world.*

*Envisioning change is not necessarily about imagining something
new; rather it is about recovering forms of thinking, being and doing
that have been ignored, devalued and erased.*

Marie-Louise Richards, 'Pedagogies of power' (2022)[5]

Economics is often talked about in terms of cycles. There are periods of
economic growth followed by stagnation and recession. Then after a time, the
economy starts growing again and the cycle repeats. It's the ebb and flow of
macroeconomics, whether one sees that as a pseudo-natural process, reflective
of political trends and policy choices, or a bit of both.

Every so often, however, there's a 'supercycle'. This is when technological
innovation reaches a critical mass and sets off an explosion leading to a new
phase of long-term economic growth. The usual business cycles still play out,
but do so within the encompassing supercycle, which over time reshapes almost
every aspect of the economy.

Architecture follows a similar pattern. This is due in part to the close
relationship between construction and the broader economy. Construction
is very often the canary in the coal mine, slowing down before an economic
slump, and then only getting going again once an economic recovery is well
underway. Although sometimes, because of the length of time it generally
takes to construct buildings, architecture and the economy can get out of
sync. This is illustrated by the fact that the Empire State Building – when
completed in 1931 – became the tallest building in the world, while the USA
was still mired in the depths of the Depression (and it maintained that status
until the topping out of the north tower of the World Trade Center in 1970).

More indirect in shaping these cycles is architecture's relationship to technology, principally the technology related to building materials and techniques. So much of the way we construct buildings is taken for granted, yet every single part of the process has been developed, adopted and become widely available at different moments in time. And each of these junctures – whether the advent of mild steel in the mid-19th century, reinforced concrete a few decades later, electrical traction elevators in the early 20th century, float glass in the 1950s, and air conditioning around this time too – have caused ripples that have reverberated long into the architectural future.

While architecture's cycles are for the most part driven by forces external to the discipline, sometimes they come from within: new agendas, new directions and new ways of thinking about and responding to the material and cultural changes of the world in which architecture is practised. Supercycles occur when the economic, technological and disciplinary coincide and align. The result, at least for the initial transitional phase, is a moment of pluralism, where no one agenda reigns supreme and multiple positions and viewpoints rise to the surface.

As was apparent at the time, as well as in retrospect, modernism was a supercycle, marked in its early days by an extraordinary pluralist culture where multiple modernisms competed and co-existed. Postmodernism was another supercycle, half a century later – a moment when stylistic pluralism once again reigned supreme. Now, half a century after that, we are going through the next supercycle.

* * *

What set the modernist supercycle apart was the implicit assertion that architecture must break free from these cyclical trajectories and instead establish one that was linear. Quite aside from Le Corbusier's polemical prognostications, we see this most explicitly in the various histories of modernism that appeared while the movement was still in its comparative infancy. Proto-histories such as Nikolaus Pevsner's *Pioneers of the Modern Movement* (1936), J.M. Richards' *An Introduction to Modern Architecture* (1940) and Sigfried Giedion's *Space, Time and Architecture: The Growth of a New Tradition* (1941) varyingly traced modernism's origins and precursors (somewhat anachronistically) to the abstract forms and truth to materials of the Arts and Crafts movement, the social concerns of William Morris, the structural honesty of Eugène Viollet-le-Duc and even the austerity of the Georgian Terrace, among other examples. Modernism was seen as the logical destination of these ideas and innovations.

Insofar as historians helped establish modernism's 'exceptionalism' in the history of architecture, it was fitting that historians were among those who led the charge against it. Among them was the Cambridge historian, David Watkin, who, hailing very much from the political right, took aim at modernism's intellectual foundation on the, in his view, false notion of the zeitgeist and its related claims to have emerged through a Hegelian notion of progress and development. Rejecting modernism's overturning of traditional styles of architecture, Watkin instead argued for the history of architecture as a series of revivals, of styles coming round again and again. And classicism, which was deemed to have been refined over its multiple revivals to a state of almost divine perfection, stood, for Watkin, at the stylistic summit.

This was not so far from a postmodernist position, though Watkin and other traditionalists abhorred its seeming triviality and infidelities. Postmodernists similarly took aim at the modernist 'project', though, unlike Watkin and his ilk, sought to replace its absolutes with relativities, and in the process open architecture up to history, memory, place, context, identity, and also – and, for some, somewhat infamously – to the market. Where modernism sought the complete transformation of the basis on which architecture was conceived and operated, postmodernism was happy to leave it as it was.

After all, it was post-*modernism* for a reason; modernism was still there. As Charles Jencks repeatedly argued, postmodernism was not modernism's repudiation – or not only that – but its transcendence. Partly for this reason, postmodernism, like modernism before it, reflects a decidedly western view of the world and of architecture's role within it. 'Regionalism' – even in its supposedly 'critical' formulation that aimed at the reconciling of modernist principles with local traditions – was woefully ill-equipped to reckon with modernism's ideologies of (imperialist) extraction and of (western) universalism.

From a theoretical perspective, one of the ironies of postmodernism's repudiation of the modernist 'grand narrative' – which was argued to be its defining contribution by one of its foremost philosophers, Jean François Lyotard – was that positing a postmodern age or postmodern condition – the title of his book – itself constituted a kind of universalism. On the ground, this could be seen playing out most visibly in the way the modernist steel and glass towers that rose in cities across the globe – irrespective of local

0.4 C.R. Cockerell, R.A., *The Professor's Dream*, 1848. A visual compendium of the great works of the history of architecture presented in a single cityscape ordered according to time, scale and location. Drawing, pencil, pen and grey ink and watercolour, with scratched highlights, 112.2 × 171.1 cm.

traditions, cultures and climates, not to mention people – carried on much the same through and beyond postmodernism.

Rather than a liberative force, architecture in this guise has merely acted as the reification of vast inequalities across the world. So often, those steel and glass towers continue to rise up at a seemingly ever-increasing rate next to or even on top of slums or public housing that has been forcibly cleared. And as significant consumers of natural resources and emitters of CO_2, they stand for the benefit of those with power and very often to the detriment of those without. This is not just an echo of colonisation, but its 21st-century practice.

Modernism held that to be radical or to 'envision change' meant looking only forward. Today, as Marie-Louise Richards so compellingly articulates, being radical is frequently about looking back – or rather, looking to what modernism and modernity ignored and frequently trampled over during its hundred-year trajectory. Revaluing traditional ways of building, local knowledges, cultures and practices are vital to foregrounding marginalised groups, perspectives and geographies.

Yet those seeking to bring about a more diverse and inclusive architecture are not alone in looking at what modernism excluded and which has largely continued to be marginalised from architecture since. Across the world, 'traditional architecture' is being co-opted by reactionary political movements and authoritarians: Trump in the USA, Modi in India and Erdogan in Turkey to name but a few.[6] Of course, in all these examples 'traditional architecture' is a very particular and selective thing, barely rooted in history and even more exclusive – culturally, socially and racially – than modernism ever was. 'Traditional architecture' is in fact little interested in tradition at all and is much more concerned with being

0.5   The history – and future – of architecture is here imagined as a spiral moving through time and space. Rather than a linear journey, styles, movements and trends wrap around one another, allowing for progress and continuity, innovation and emulation, with the past enriching the future and the future re-conceiving the past.

able to use architecture as an instrument of the assertion of power and authority, which at its most extreme becomes avowedly nativist and unashamedly racist.

Thus, the challenge becomes one of articulating an architecture that is progressive, but which can draw from the architectural past; that looks beyond universalist narratives of modernisation while recognising that this project carried with it an immutable belief in the value of democracy, the rule of law and human rights. Squaring this circle requires rethinking the trajectory of architecture so that it is neither linear nor cyclical but both at the same time: as a spiral moving through space. Thus, rather than an inexorable journey to some predefined destination, or the endless and exclusionary repetition of so-called traditions, architecture's stylistic oscillations are given impetus and direction, so that the past is constantly in the process of being re-examined, re-worked and re-energised by the present, and vice versa.

This in itself is nothing new. While architecture is undoubtedly – and in many ways inescapably – a reflection of economics, capital and power, it is never just that. Over history, the best architecture has always transcended its origins, indeed time itself, manifesting different things simultaneously. In order to find ways towards, and making space for, those architectures, it is vital to seize the opportunities brought about by the present 'supercycle' to articulate new inclusive and progressive agendas for the next 50 years. To do so requires further exploration of the mechanisms that shape such moments of transition, the ways in which pluralist architectural cultures arise through them, and how, moreover, they might be sustained.

Usually in architectural history, different approaches wax and wane in opposition. But every now and then, when the economic and cultural conditions are right, there is a sudden, mutual flowering of different traditions, just as in evolutionary history there can be a simultaneous explosion of new species all prospering for a time. This can be conceived, visually, as the expanding end of a trumpet.

My preference is that it [postmodernism] remain one voice among many – that it not dominate a city or culture ... True postmodernists believe in a field of tensions, in the necessity for Traditional and Modernist approaches to flourish, in order to sustain all their meanings.

Charles Jencks, 'Death for Rebirth' (1990)[7]

During the 1990s, the political thinker Joseph P. Overton postulated that a policy's political viability depended on whether it falls within the range of what is deemed acceptable by the public. If a policy falls inside the Overton window, as it was posthumously named, then it is likely to be looked upon favourably, enter mainstream discourse and stand a good chance of being enacted. If, in contrast, a policy falls near the window's edge or, perhaps even beyond it, then it will be seen as radical, unacceptable to the mainstream and consequently disregarded.

Architecture has an Overton window too, one that similarly acts to regulate what is permissible at any given moment – though, of course, in a very different register to politics. Architecture generally operates more abstractly, with its Overton window widening, not according to the poles of left and right, but between permissiveness and order, between moments of stylistic experimentation, individuality and innovation, and moments when conformance reigns supreme.

Although architecture and politics are tightly interwoven, the architectural Overton window does not follow the political one; when one is open it does not necessarily mean the other is too. There are points of intersection and correlation, but, as we have seen, architecture tends to have a closer alignment to economics, so for the majority of the time the political and architectural

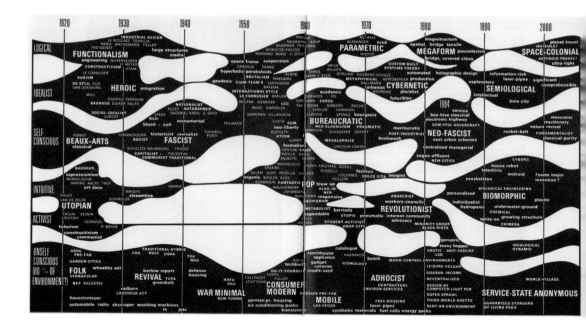

Overton windows follow asynchronous trajectories. To elucidate this idea further, and explore its implications for the present moment, we will look back to look forward, to the aforementioned previous 'supercycle' when the architectural Overton window opened wide: postmodernism.

* * *

One of the very many striking things about flicking through the first edition of Charles Jencks' seminal *The Language of Post-Modern Architecture* (1977) is how little postmodern architecture it actually contains. The book went through so many editions that it is easy to forget just how pioneering the early ones were. It is telling that Minoru Takeyama's Ni-Ban-Kahn in Shinjuku, Tokyo (1970) adorns the cover, undoubtedly an important project but not one that would now generally be regarded as one of postmodernism's more canonical examples. While initially there was not yet enough postmodernism to fill the book's pages, by the time later editions were published, it had become the era's dominant architectural force.

In architecture, discourse generally runs ahead of design at least as far as it is manifested in actual building. And so, at the height of postmodern 'building', postmodern discourse was no longer in the ascendant; in fact, a case could reasonably be made that whatever radical edge postmodernism had possessed disappeared the moment Philip Johnson appeared on the

0.6 The 'Evolutionary Tree' is Charles Jencks' attempt at capturing the various impulses, tendencies and ideals that drove architectural production. This earlier version was published in his book, *Architecture 2000: Predictions and Methods* (1971), Jencks reworked the diagram numerous times (these annotations are c.1999) over the next five decades.

cover of *Time* magazine clutching a model of his AT&T building. This marked the moment postmodernism went mainstream, with the result that it lost its claim of being radical, but with the corollary that its impact on the world had increased massively.

In terms of the implications of all this on the opening (and closing) of the architectural Overton window – and its consequent effects on architectural culture – there is a cumulative effect, so that, to continue with the example of postmodernism, in its early days at least, each postmodern building made it easier for the next and so on. The AT&T building would have been impossible without James Stirling's Neue Staatsgalerie, which itself would have been very hard to accomplish without Robert Venturi's Vanna Venturi House, and so on. In this way, what was once thought to be on the margins of acceptability later becomes mainstream, with early outliers playing an important role in making what follows seem less extreme and thereby allowing the architectural Overton window to open.

All styles are to a greater or lesser extent conceived in opposition to what came before. Postmodernism emerged in response to the aesthetic and ideological dead end that modernism found itself in by the 1970s. Where the conformity of late modernism had kept the architectural window only slightly ajar – to put it crudely though not wholly unfairly, mandating steel and glass International Style for commercial buildings and Brutalism for public ones – postmodernism opened the window to the fresh, pluralist air. It was only natural that once that fresh air had done its work, the window would close again and, as would transpire during the 1990s, the postmodern impulse (and related style) would fall from favour.

This trajectory is far from unique to postmodernism, of course. Every architectural movement follows a similar cycle: youthful radical vigour, mainstream maturity and then inevitable decline. Thus after the permissiveness of postmodernism, there was a reversion to a kind of neo-modernism(s), a recapitulation of modernist aesthetics yet shorn of their ideological underpinnings. But where the avant-garde had served as the driver of modernist progress, what emerged during the 1990s was an architectural culture pushing in lots of different directions – forward, but also back, sideways, and at different speeds – with little sense of any one agenda taking the broader discipline with it or at least laying out a path to be followed.

This has led, since that moment, to a period of extraordinary fragmentation of aesthetic experience, aided and abetted, from the 2000s onwards, by

structural changes in architectural media. The age of the journal as the principal means for the dissemination of architectural discourse has given way to blogs and now to social media where the image reigns supreme over other forms of media or discourse. This decentralisation has been hugely beneficial in allowing a much broader range of projects and architects to achieve prominence than would have been allowed or possible under old media, destabilising existing hierarchies and giving platforms to a much larger number of voices. Yet it has also ensured that it is now all but impossible to make sense of contemporary architectural production. Previous categorising concepts no longer apply. Chief among these is the concept of style which had arisen in the late 19th century to a large degree as a consequence of the advent of photography and the ability it allowed, for the first time in human history, to place two buildings side by side and in that comparison discern common or differentiating characteristics from which one might construct different styles. However, the present proliferation of images on social media render such binary comparisons moot and the concept of style redundant. Thus architecture today is defined not by style, but by its extraordinary, unprecedented variety.

But these structural changes in architectural media – which on one level could be seen as simply the latest example of phenomena that have occurred multiple times over history – are only part of the story. As critiques from the political left have long pointed out, the retreat of the public sector in most western economies that began in the late 1970s and early 1980s, and four decades of subsequent free-market policies – variously described as neoliberalism – has seen architecture increasingly financialised, becoming in some guises little more than an instrument of capital. But what those critiques have often overlooked is the way that this financialisation has been assisted by the fragmentation of architectural culture (and of culture more broadly) and the aesthetic chaos that has ensued. From being not long ago a discipline and creative endeavour that had a clear sense of its power and potential, architecture today has become so fragmented that any kind of shared ideal or mission seems hopelessly naive. Thus it became easy prey for market forces.

In the same way that Charles Jencks, nearly five decades ago, saw modernism as limiting the possibilities of architecture's stylistic expression, so its present financialisation and instrumentalisation towards the needs of capital is increasingly tending towards a meaningless, moribund and one-

0.7 Begun in 2010 by Andrew Kovacs, 'Archive of Affinities is a constantly updated collection of architectural images ... [It] is not an archive of the canon or of tradition, but rather of the overlooked; or the Architectural B-side ... arranged in multiple ways to become a crucible for making architecture from architecture.' https://o-k-o-k.net/ARCHIVE-OF-AFFINITIES.

dimensional architecture. Infinite aesthetic variety has become a mask for declining agency.

Today, architecture has become so undifferentiated and atomised that, as in the political sphere, shared or common meanings from which new collective agendas emerge seemingly no longer exist. This is a problem not just for architecture itself, but for the role it plays in establishing and rooting the social and cultural ties that prevent society itself from fragmenting and drifting apart – a role that has never been more important given the polarisation of political debate across the world. Architecture needs, once again, to become a physical and metaphorical meeting place where we come together as individuals and as a public, where reactionary fragmentation is replaced by a progressive pluralism. The question is how – which the next sections aim to address.

In architecture particularly, the dominant voice has historically been a singular, exclusive voice, whose reach and power ignores huge swathes of humanity – financially, creatively, conceptually – as though we have been listening and speaking in one tongue only. The 'story' of architecture is therefore incomplete. Not wrong, but incomplete. It is in this context particularly that exhibitions matter. They are a unique moment in which to augment, change, or re-tell a story, whose audience and impact is felt far beyond the physical walls and spaces that hold it. What we say publicly matters because it is the ground on which change is built, in tiny increments as well as giant leaps.

Lesley Lokko, *The Laboratory of the Future* (2023)[8]

0.8   Installation shot showing a model of the Villa Savoye installed at the *Modern Architecture: International Exhibition* at the Museum of Modern Art, New York, 1932. Curated by Henry-Russell Hitchcock and Philip Johnson, the exhibition popularised modernist architecture in the USA, but erased many of its points of differentiation.

Curatorial projects – whether exhibitions, events such as those from which this book derives, workshops or symposia, to mention just a few of the most obvious formats – have long acted as forums for meeting and debating new, progressive ideas. From the *Modern Architecture: International Exhibition* at New York's Museum of Modern Art in 1932, to *The Presence of the Past*, the first Venice Architecture Biennale in 1980 (which brought postmodernism to the world stage), and indeed to Lesley Lokko's *Laboratory of the Future,* the 18th biennale held in 2023, exhibitions have long been spaces where architectural culture is made manifest, bringing the otherwise disparate and fragmented into proximity where shared meanings and common agendas can be formed – which is a good definition of a culture of pluralism.

With the decline of magazines and journals, curatorial projects have become all the more important in articulating new directions and ways of thinking. Also vital – and this is sometimes levelled as a criticism – is that they are distinct from architecture as building, though they do sometimes encompass that. Instead, they constitute the cultural space of architecture, where discourse is formed and takes place, generally away from the world of practice. These curatorial spaces are where architecture exists as a discipline as opposed to a profession.

It is no coincidence that each of the exhibitions cited above coincides with supercycles when the Overton window was wide open. In their own ways, each were attempts to channel and direct these moments of transition and flux towards progressive ideals and aspirations. Yet, in the case of the first two

0.9   The centrepiece of the 1980 Venice Architecture Biennale – the first to be held devoted to architecture – was the Strada Novissima, a kind of street-as-collage where a range of architects were invited to create facades reflecting their own interests and concerns, whilst appearing collectively under the postmodernist banner.

0.10   Created for
the central pavilion
of the 2023 Venice
Architecture Biennale,
Olalekan Jeyifous's
AAP/ACE, 2023
imagines an alternate
history/future where
the ecological damage
inflicted on Africa
during colonisation
is reversed via a pan-
African movement
utilising indigenous
knowledge to create
renewable energy
systems.

examples, they also demonstrated the way radical positions can, despite their intentions, often be made to serve, despite their intentions, in the validation of the mainstream.

In the case of *Modern Architecture*, the exhibition itself was complicit in this process, taking the competition of styles that defined early modernism and subsuming them into a single, ostensibly universal 'International Style'. Even if the postmodernism biennale 50 years later did not seek to codify the movement to the same extent, and was inherently more pluralist in spirit, it did help serve it up to be appropriated by commercial forces over the following years. And fast forwarding to the present, the risk for any curatorial project is that they similarly end up inadvertently helping to legitimise the practices they aim to overturn.

* * *

The role that radical or progressive ideas and practices play in relation to mainstream architectural culture is frequently a counterintuitive one. To elucidate it further we might draw, however improbably, from the ideas of the philosopher Jacques Derrida, in particular his notion of the supplement – the seemingly insignificant part of something that is actually vital to the integrity of the whole. The supplement is used here to open up new ways of thinking about the structure of the architectural discipline via a short discussion of two celebrated groups of practitioners whose work stands on the edge and sometimes beyond what is conventionally considered architecture.

The first group is Forensic Architecture, who have achieved wide recognition in recent years, and were an intriguing inclusion among the four nominees for the 2018 Turner Prize – a prize that recognises leading *artists* in the UK. Founded at Goldsmiths, University of London, in 2011, Forensic Architecture's self-declared mission is to 'undertake advanced architectural and media research on behalf of international prosecutors, human rights organisations and political and environmental justice groups'.[9]

Forensic Architecture describe their work as 'counter-forensics', as opposed to 'forensics' which is carried out by state actors. In the era of 'fake news', they see their painstaking analytical approach as a vital tool in holding authorities to account. While operating in a vastly expanded disciplinary field – the collective

0.11   This image was created by Forensic Architecture as part of their investigation of the kidnapping of an Israeli soldier by Hamas during the 2014 Gaza conflict which resulted in four days of bombardment. Denied entry to the Gaza Strip, FA relied on the examination of images and videos shared online. https://forensic-architecture.org/investigation/the-bombing-of-rafah.

involves architects, filmmakers, lawyers and scientists – they still consider their highly politically motivated practice to be a form of architecture. This is not simply about using certain architectural techniques, but drawing from architecture's ability to synthesise different disciplines to work on the behalf of civil society.

Perhaps not coincidentally, Forensic Architecture were not the first architectural practitioners to be nominated for the Turner Prize. The celebrated, multi-disciplinary, though very much architecturally rooted, collective, Assemble, were themselves nominated and won the prize in 2015. While Assemble and Forensic Architecture operate almost in two separate worlds, they have interesting similarities: their more or less overt social and political agendas, their constitution as collectives rather than conventional hierarchical organisations, and the fact that their work exists on the margins of the architectural discipline – and technically speaking, outside of the architectural profession. And to this we might add, the fact that they also regularly exhibit their work.

Both groups clearly see the vital role that exhibitions play in creating spaces for alternative architectural agendas. Yet that focus on exhibitions has a bigger role, offering ways to reach beyond the usual architectural echo chamber. For Forensic Architecture, exhibiting is a crucial means of presenting their research unmediated, directly to the public. For Assemble too, it is clearly of a piece with their participatory form of architecture that involves end-users in all stages of the architectural process.

This explicit connection to the public is interesting because it is something that is still claimed for the architectural profession as a whole – the concern for the public good being what supposedly distinguishes architecture from other disciplines in the building construction industry. Forty years ago, when around half of architects in the UK, for example, worked in the public sector, what this meant was easier to define (even if the reality was often rather more complex). Today, we can look at much of what is done in the name of architecture amid the discipline's almost total financialisation and wonder where this public spirit has gone.

It's here that we come back to Derrida and the supplement. With the supplement in mind, we can see that the work of Forensic Architecture, Assemble and others is not marginal or incidental to the mainstream architectural profession, but is actually supplemental to it, vital to its integrity and self-image. The overtly socially and politically engaged work of these groups serves to demonstrate that architecture is not just the second oldest profession, willing to prostrate itself to satisfy the needs of the client, but is concerned with the public good, and stands outside and for something other than market forces, even though – and this is the crucial point – most of the profession does not. Forensic Architecture, Assemble and other groups working on architecture's margins stand out because of how closed-off the broader profession has become.

All this is not to argue that Forensic Architecture and Assemble constitute particular models to be followed, or even that their respective outlooks and practices should necessarily be endorsed; neither is unproblemmatic or without inconsistencies and contradictions. Rather, their example is used to ask the fundamental question of how the avowed concern for the public and civil society that distinguishes their work and other studios and practitioners like them might seep back into the broader profession. This is not about the supplement infiltrating the whole, which would leave the disciplinary formation intact, but how we can break the supplementary relationship entirely, and ensure the margins no longer allow the centre to maintain its destructive values and practices.

The answer to this question, this book argues, lies in fostering a culture of pluralism, one that vitally abolishes the centre-margin relationship. A pluralist architecture is polycentric, it is an architecture of multiple voices, positions and perspectives that at the same time converse and interact: not a new architecture, but another architecture.

* * *

This is what the present book aims, albeit in a modest way, to help bring about. It is not a manifesto but a platform – one that brings together twelve contributions from practitioners, researchers, educators and curators, who are each working at pushing architecture in different directions, and in the process rethinking what architecture can be and what it can do. While the contributors' respective practices, approaches and outlooks might conventionally appear as disconnected from each other as they are from architecture's centre, here they are presented as part of a disciplinary continuum.

The book is split into four sections. The first – *Knowledges* – considers the bodies of knowledge that define how we understand architecture and its role in the world. Senegalese architect, Nzinga Biegueng Mboup, discusses how the work of her practice, Worofila, draws from local traditions and practices to define an inclusive form of architectural modernity. Hungarian architect Dávid Smiló reflects on the architectural inheritances that shape young architects' cultural formation – what is foregrounded and what is excluded – and the broader role of past architectures in activating present ones. Then, Anab Jain and Jon Ardern, of the ideas and design studio, Superflux, explore how they conjure visceral experiences that offer new ways of understanding the world and our place in it, culminating with a manifesto for bringing about a 'more-than-human' future.

Sites, the second section, explores the expanding fields in which architecture now operates, and the practices and perspectives required to work in them. Xu Tiantian explores the work of her practice, DnA_Design and Architecture, in Songyang County, Zhejiang province, China, and the approaches it has fashioned towards creating contemporary rural architecture, in part as a counterpoint to the country's unprecedented period of urbanisation. Curator and educator, Gonzalo Herrero Delicado, argues for the emergence of a 'liquid architecture' that is attuned to both the challenges and opportunities presented by the emergence of new immersive digital worlds. The critic, Marianela D'Aprile, argues for writing as a vital site of architectural production, where the forces driving construction – practical, economic, ideological – can be made manifest and enter public, as well as professional, discourse.

The new disciplinary formations necessary to bring about another architecture are not just about remaking architecture from the inside out, but also from the outside in. This means forming new *Alliances* that extend across disciplines, fields and publics. Ruth Morrow explores the range of collaborations and collaborative practices that have emerged in her work with biomaterials at Queen's University Belfast and now at Newcastle University. Alice Brownfield considers the intersections of architecture and activism that are necessary to bring about a more equitable built environment – both in physical form and the social and cultural structures and relations that it supports and reflects. Researcher and educator, Xenia Adjoubei, presents FIELD, a collaborative bio-arts platform that develops new materials and ways of making to posit alternative approaches to land ownership, ecology and urbanism.

Architecture is complicit in perpetuating the injustices that plague the contemporary world – not simply in the way architecture is used or by whom, but in its very philosophical and disciplinary make-up. *Resets*, the

0.12   Le Corbusier's Villa Savoye in Poissy, on the edge of Paris (1928–31), is in many ways the archetype of first generation modernist ideals. Simultaneously employing and embodying Le Corbusier's 'five points' prescription for modernist architecture, the house was as much manifesto as dwelling.

final section of the book, considers the need for rethinking the foundations of architecture. Practitioner, researcher and educator, V. Mitch McEwen, explores the entanglements of architecture, climate destruction and race, sharing 'building with' as a Black paradigm for creating space in the midst of mutual aid and care. London-based researcher and designer, Marianna Janowicz, focuses on the home as site of radical action towards dismantling the patriarchal systems and processes that define architecture – as well as the broader world. Finally, the academic, Joshua Mardell, and artist-designer, Adam Nathaniel Furman, explore, first, the exclusion of queer experiences and perspectives from the history of architecture, while, second, arguing for a 'queer architecture' as a rebuke to or refusal of any kind of order or linear progress.

Books tend for the most part to be the culmination or summation of a project or body or work. We hope that this book will be the opposite, acting as a spur or catalyst for action to bring about a progressive, inclusive architecture, one that operates as an instrument of liberation, empowerment and transformation. When Le Corbusier asked, a hundred years ago, whether the future would bring 'architecture or revolution', it was not the answer he got wrong but the question itself. Today, we see that it is not architecture or revolution that is needed, but architecture *and* revolution.

KNOWLEDGES

1

LEARNING FROM THE VERNACULAR IN SENEGAL

THE ARCHITECTURE OF WOROFILA

Nzinga Biegueng Mboup

There are just over 200 registered architects practising in Senegal today, which in part explains why 93 per cent of construction projects in Dakar are done without the involvement of an architect.[1]

Establishing oneself as an architect in Senegal poses the double onus of having to operate within a context that builds without architects but also one where architecture is the only profession within the built environment that is regulated and carries legal responsibilities, such as building safety and adherence to planning laws. Beyond architects' legal responsibilities are those that extend to making architecture that responds to the needs and culture of Senegalese society.[2]

Senegal is in the middle of a construction boom, spearheaded by the previous administration that set a trend for a series of colossal projects, monuments, new cities, stadia and road infrastructures intended to mark the country's 'emergence'. Concrete, glass, steel and aluminium are the materials of choice for this 'emerging' architecture that for most is a leap towards modernity. Projects such as Diamniadio Lake City – a vast, futuristic new town 30 km from Dakar, the country's capital – exemplify this in appearing to have been conceived with little concern for the Senegalese context. Such high-carbon projects are being developed against the backdrop of an increasing awareness of our over-dependence on fossil fuels and resulting urgent need to shift towards decarbonisation. Buildings account for 39 per cent of global carbon emissions,[3] and in Senegal, cement alone was responsible for 17 per cent of emissions in 2019.[4]

It is against this backdrop that Worofila, the architectural practice I co-founded with Nicolas Rondet, emerged four years ago with the aim of

1.1 Worofila, Keru Mbuubenne, Sendou, Senegal, 2021.

promoting a bioclimatic approach to architecture and cities. Our design approach is informed by the climatic and socio-economic contexts in which we work. We prioritise building with biomaterials that can be found locally and require little energy in the processes of transformation. This is made possible in Senegal through a wealth of resources at our disposal which we use to define a much more sustainable and contextual, yet experimental, modern architecture.

LEARNING FROM THE VERNACULAR

Worofila's approach emerged from the belief that the resources used to define modernity in Senegalese architecture can be found in the local knowledge and ancestral techniques of construction that have stood the test of time and which show a deep understanding of the country's ecosystems. Throughout regions of Senegal and the Sahel region, one can find countless examples of grand vernacular buildings made out of earth and, particularly, clay. The Great Mosque of Djenné in Mali (originally 13th-century; rebuilt 1908) is a prime example of a building that exemplifies the dramatic scale that earth-built structures can achieve, while the yearly maintenance of the facade reinforces the idea of buildings emerging from collective efforts and an attention to natural cycles, with clay mined from the river when it is at its lowest and used to protect the building before the start of the rainy season.

Raw earth construction techniques – mostly of adobe mud bricks and known as 'banco' – are utilised throughout the Sahel. In Senegal these techniques still exist in the regions of the Fouta, home to the Omarian Mosques, and in Casamance, known for its impluvium houses in which earthen walls made with cob are topped by the double-sided roof which collects rainwater in the atrium (fig.1.2).

The lessons from all these vernacular buildings are in the use of materials available in close proximity, be they wood, vegetal fibres, clay or cow dung. These local materials then become building components through the actions of a local workforce trained by their predecessors to make buildings that respond to the climatic conditions, the constraints of each material and the way in which people live. This way of approaching design and construction is contextual and sustainable as the predominant biomaterials used have low embodied energy and are assembled in a way that requires very little

1.2 Worofila, Earthen cob house under construction in Casamance, Senegal, 2021.

energy during the operational stage. They can be easily recycled or even reused when the building is no longer required and is demolished.

USING BIOMATERIALS IN AN INNOVATIVE WAY

In today's Senegal, the palette of biomaterials used for construction are predominantly earth/clay as well as vegetal fibres of multiple origins. Laterite is abundant in the vicinity of Dakar and in the north and south of the country, with other clay-rich earths found close to the vicinity of rivers. Laterite has been used for centuries in construction, with the earliest examples being the megaliths of Senegambia made out of cut laterite blocks. Nowadays, laterite rock is pulverised and compressed manually to form stabilised earth blocks that are sun dried before being used for masonry construction.

Earthen bricks can be used in a variety of ways, though because they work well in compression are particularly useful in making load-bearing walls, as well as other self-supporting structural elements like arches, vaults and

1.3   Worofila, photograph showing construction methods for the NKD House, Dakar, Senegal, 2021.

1.4   Worofila, NKD House, Dakar, Senegal, 2021.

domes. Structural earthen walls have to be thicker than the equivalent concrete block walls, and the increased thickness creates more thermal inertia to the buildings, allowing them to have better thermal regulation during day and night. At Worofila, we have placed an emphasis on assembling bricks in a way that expresses their unique materiality whilst remaining functional. On the Keru Mbuubene project and Project NKD (figs 1.1, 1.3 and 1.4) the brick courses alternate in size, with one brick course overhanging by a few centimetres, acting as a brise-soleil and casting shadows on the wall, further protecting it from insolation.

1.5 and 1.6
Worofila, Eco Pavilion,
Diamniadio, Senegal,
2019.

Wood is a scarce resource in Senegal where some forests are protected against illegal tree-cutting. However, vegetal fibres are varied, and one particular weed called typha has proven to provide enormous benefits for construction. *Typha* is a plant belonging to the genus of *Typhaceae* that grows on river banks (predominantly the river Senegal) and has insulation properties similar to those of hemp. The reed can be used for charcoal-making, thatch roofing and more recently insulating building blocks. Typha, when crushed and mixed with clay, can form beam blocks used for roof slab construction, adobe blocks that can be used for masonry, or simply to create a plaster where the fibres help stabilise the clay content that can easily crack when drying. Worofila has experimented with typha in many of its projects, using it for wall and roof insulation in various ways. In the eco pavilion of Diamniadio (figs 1.5, 1.6), a dry and simply woven reed thatch was placed on the external walls of an adobe building, while inside, cut panels were placed on a ceiling grid, acting as sound absorption panels to improve acoustics.

Using such readily available materials which require little energy for transformation reflects our belief in the value of building materials that are low-tech, non-polluting and can be recycled or transformed and used in ways that create thermal and physiological comfort for the user and building occupant. It is important to note that although the use of biomaterials contributes greatly to reducing the carbon footprint of the construction, it is vital that the design and layout of the building aligns and responds to solar orientation, the direction of winds and the general context of the site. Given the generally tropical, dry climate of Senegal, this can be easily achieved by applying key principles of bioclimatic design.

THE BIOCLIMATIC APPROACH

Worofila's approach to bioclimatic architecture draws inspiration from vernacular architecture in its use of materials, but at the same time seeks ways to adapt them to the realities of current socio-economic contexts. A good example of this approach is Project NKD, a four-and-a-half storey home in Dakar.

On a compact plot of 150 sqm, with one street-facing facade to the north-east, Worofila designed a structure comprising 420 sqm spread across four-and-a-half floors and organised around two atria: one that contained a swimming pool and the other a patio adjacent to the stairwell that acts as a light and ventilation well. Most of the floor plates are cross-ventilated to allow for passive cooling, and openings are large enough to provide natural lighting (fig.1.7). Ceiling fans are the predominant mechanical cooling devices during the hot and humid months, with the electrical supply powered by solar panels on the roof terraces.

The openings of the envelope are carefully placed on the north-eastern facade and the atria, while half of the southern facade and the western facade are windowless. Traditional buildings in Senegal have very few openings on the outside which helps to limit the entry of sunlight and heat; any small openings that are present are to allow for natural ventilation.

We are becoming increasingly aware of the importance of live trees and plants in creating shade and also conferring micro-climates through transpiration. Senegal is dotted with endemic plants such as some acacias that are suited to the amount of water available in our tropical, dry ecosystems. Culturally speaking, trees have also marked the sites of gathering and increase the quality of outdoor spaces. So, the fact that the building is formed from formerly living material – earth and typha – is a way of making its users and inhabitants feel at ease, physiologically and culturally.

1.7   Diagrams of strategies for passive cooling and natural lighting for NKD house, 2023.

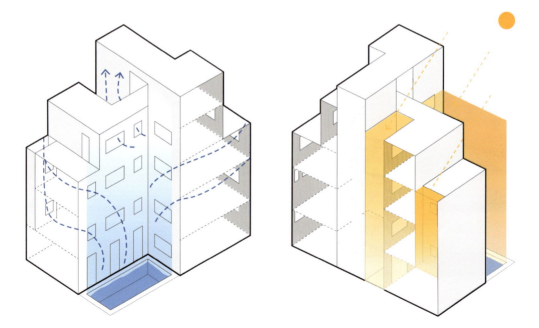

1.8 Brick course mock-ups for NKD House, Dakar, Senegal, 2020.

ON COLLABORATIVE PRACTICES

Being able to experiment and innovate by constantly finding new ways to use and define existing materials is made possible by collaboration with various actors on the ground, from building material factories to local artisans.

Our introduction to compressed earth blocks and to typha came about through a visit to the Elementerre factory outside Dakar. It was founded by Doudou Deme, an engineer trained in Craterre who wanted to prove that we could build using ancestral techniques present in houses that he, like many others, inhabited when growing up. Deme operates as a supplier of many bio-based construction materials such as adobes and typha insulation panels and also works as a builder for projects using traditional and modern mud construction techniques, including many Worofila projects. The Elementerre factory also functions as a laboratory where we have been able to customise a lot of products made there for various projects: from mixing various types of sand and clay-rich soil to obtain a variation of colours in natural bricks, to developing custom-sized bricks to fit the details of projects such as Keru Mbuubenne or Project NKD (fig.1.8).

The streets of Dakar are packed with independent artisans making bespoke products on a daily basis; carpenters, tailors, welders, weavers and others are constantly at work, giving local people, as well as designers, easy access to expert craftsmanship. At Worofila, we have partnered with ceramicists to produce weatherproof artisanal tiles and gutter spouts for use on several projects. We have also worked with a weaving company that uses natural materials such as palm fibres to help us improve the *typha* woven panels that we have experimented with as wall cladding and ceiling materials. Lastly, carpenters and wood-workers have become allies in allowing us to make interior furniture and custom-made windows and doors for houses.

Our working relationship with these artisans, manufacturers and masons follows a process of trial and error, requiring the architect to spend time on site and to learn to communicate creatively, not only through drawings, but also mock-ups. Learning from skilled craftsmen also helps us understand the properties of material better, and in return we motivate the craftspeople to produce novel typologies and expand the applications of their work.

DEMOCRATISING THE PROCESS

Whilst concrete, steel, glass and aluminium are still the dominant materials of new construction in Senegal, there is a growing interest in passive design and earth construction as more people rediscover their cooling benefits, evident from the examples of traditional architecture. To effect meaningful change, this awareness has to be accompanied by an ecosystem that can support these types of construction, which requires training and larger supply chains. Construction sites can become places of learning and transmission of knowledge, especially when it comes to building in urban areas where earth construction is a skill that has sadly been forgotten. There is a cumulative effect, so that masons who have acquired the skills of building an earth dome, for instance, pass them on through repeating the task with new masons, while we as architects get to adapt our designs to reflect the expertise of the craftspeople we work with. We see it as a vital part of our work to disseminate knowledge and expand the number of qualified masons and suppliers of these bio-based materials so they are available to everyone, which is especially important for a country such as Senegal where auto-construction is still prevalent.

DEFINING SENEGALESE ARCHITECTURAL MODERNITY

The latest Senegalese law on architecture of March 2021 states that 'the use of built space should be in line with the needs and aspirations of the African society, following its unique genius and culture', but this is yet to be defined in any significant way.[5] The modern history of Senegal has been marked by projects led by foreign agents such as the Dakar Trade Fair. Built in 1974 in the north of the city, the Dakar Trade Fair was designed by two young French architects, Jean-Louis Marin and Jean-François Lamoureux, who created a set of pyramidal and triangular structures which answered the first Senegalese president, Leopold Sedar Senghor's call for a new national style of architecture based on fractal geometry and called 'Asymmetrical Parallelism'.[6]

For all their formal and structural bravado – and in many ways because of it – these projects have been dominated by cement which, although produced locally, remains a polluting and high-carbon material that results in buildings that require air conditioning. The emphasis on using local resources and making passive buildings that respond to the socio-cultural and climatic context is a step towards a low-carbon future while simultaneously supporting and drawing from the development of local industries, local skills and collective 'genius'. In the new era of 'emergence', we are passionate believers in the possibility of Senegalese architectural modernity that encompasses simplicity, sustainability, contextuality and originality by drawing inspiration from our heritage, and thus responding to our current situation without jeopardising the futures of following generations.

2

ONE STEP BACK, TWO STEPS FORWARD

PLURALISM, POST-MODERNISM AND ARCHITECTURE IN THE CLIMATE EMERGENCY

Dávid Smiló

During our time as architecture students at the Budapest Technological University in the early 2010s, we found ourselves repeatedly drawn to Hungarian architecture magazines and publications from the 1970s and 1980s. We sought out as many as we could find from the shelves of both online and offline second-hand bookshops. These publications, which appeared during the last years of the declining socialist era, had a unique aesthetic quality – albeit paralleled by international trends, although this was partly what made them unique in Hungary – which helped create a liberated milieu in an otherwise closed and limited socialist culture and society.

In these publications we found works by architects whom we have known, in some cases even personally as our professors, or as important individuals of the Hungarian architectural world. But we were entirely unfamiliar with their works from the 1970s and 1980s: projects such as the atelier house of László Rajk and Bálint Nagy, György Kévés' architecture, works of Dezső Ekler and the organic movement, the early houses of Mihály Balázs and Tamás Karácsony, community centres around the country designed by Péter Reimholz, and the astounding scenery created by Attila F. Kovács.

We found ourselves looking at houses, installations, exhibitions and productions of building camps that had not formed part of the academic nor the wider professional discourse. It seemed as if they were not only forgotten but perhaps something to be ashamed of.

The projects revealed a very particular type of aesthetic and design approach, often abundant in both architectural fantasy and contradictions.

2.1 House from Grandma's Curtain is a concept building as a part of the No Place House series, 2021.

They showed the frequent use of circles, quarters of a circle, triangles, the dominance of geometrical compositions of facades, an emphasis on graphic design in the floor plan, expressive representation techniques, artistic fetishism of drawings, classicism and eclecticism, yet all rendered through a socialist implementation and a culture and economy of shortage, which resulted in slightly imperfect arches, limited materials and an occasionally disrupted geometric order.

This unusual state of absence or even erasure of what, in our eyes, was a vital part of Hungarian architectural culture led us to do two things. First, as members of the student studio of the Budapest Technological University, we organised a course to reveal the architectural life of the 1980s. During this we realised the lack of documentation of this period (in addition to its absence in media) and decided to conduct interviews with some of the individuals mentioned above.

Our confusion further rose when we obtained many editions of *The Japan Architect* and *Architectural Design* from the 1980s and 1990s. While going through these editions we realised that the Hungarian architectural culture with which we were so enamoured wasn't the only one abundant in works that had been erased from our shared memory, but that the same had happened in international architecture as well.

Years later, in 2016, we founded Paradigma Ariadné, and it quickly became clear that we were not the only young architects with a sensitivity towards the aesthetic and intellectual environment of another period. We were lucky, in a sense, that we had been able to recognise it so early. Our discovery of this international peer group was made possible in part by the advent of social media. We were now able to see and follow up in real time what was happening in other emerging architecture studios. We saw that we had not been alone in taking an interest in and drawing inspiration from this moment in architectural culture, which we can simply refer to as postmodern architecture. A large group of architects who were attracted to aesthetic innovation jumped straight into the *floating gap* of architecture. But what exactly was happening and why?

For us, it came down to architecture's representations in digital media. Modernism is now a hundred years old and even its post-war iterations have long been subject to concerted historical study. Modernism has become an historical style like any other. At the same time, since at least the 1990s and in some instances before, attention has turned to the question of heritage protection and management of a growing number of modernist buildings. The result of all

2.2 A buffalo barn and an educational trail in rural Hungary rethink the aesthetic of the buildings of industrialised agriculture, 2021.

this is that there is a vast amount of material – from academic articles to simple images – about modernist architecture online, accessible anywhere, anytime at the click of a button.

The digital revolution was, of course, not limited to the consumption of discourse and media but also reshaped its production. Digitalisation fundamentally changed the landscape of contemporary architectural production, beginning in the late 1990s, getting into its stride in the early 2000s and accelerating ever since. The result is that today we can access within seconds images and drawings of buildings created after the 2000s. Offices that want to be represented and visible are part of a giant sea of architectural images, which – albeit only in theory – are accessible to all. I say only in theory, because in the context of the vast sea of image culture accelerated by digitalisation, the question is no longer whether you can be a drop in the ocean, but whether that drop can be a unique, traceable one. Naturally, the most striking or highest quality images rise to the top, which is only partly related to quality or significance of the project being depicted.

Between the moment when modern architecture was taking its last breath in the early 1970s, and the advent of the first fully digitalised architecture

in the late 1990s, lies the 30 or 40 years of postmodernism when journals and magazines were the chief vehicles for the transmission of architectural media. In addition to the well-known titles already mentioned above, these printed magazines included less well-known papers that were the subject of the influential exhibition *Clip/Stamp/Fold: The Radical Architecture of Little Magazines 196X–197X* first shown at the Storefront for Art and Architecture in New York in November 2006 before touring widely.

When we were students, and in many instances still today, this vast corpus has one very important attribute distinguishing it from what came before and after: its content cannot be accessed through clicks. If you want to know what these magazines contained and to find out more about what took place in the architecture of those decades of the 20th century, then you have to do what otherwise seemed rather strange after the 2000s and arguably even stranger now: you go to the library.

We knew about the Piazza d'Italia, about Venturi, and also about the role played by Emilio Ambasz. We were aware that the books of Charles Jencks provided a good summary of all that happened before the 1990s. However, it soon became apparent that the accuracy of our knowledge of postmodernist architecture is comparable to the understanding of the universe provided by the Hubble Space Telescope. All hunky-dory, but if you entered the library and opened the magazines of that period, you felt like the astronomer who looks into the James Webb Telescope having switched from the Hubble. The faded spots

2.3   Open air exhibition place for twelve images, 2022.

among the glittering galaxies hide thousands of other galaxies. Postmodernist architecture seemed to be infinite.

If the above provides an explanation for how a generation shifted from one aesthetic vocabulary to another in a structural sense, the question of why we and others absorbed postmodern architecture and tried to reinterpret it within the context of our own period with such zest remains. Why, one could reasonably ask, are we doing this in a world that is heading toward a climate catastrophe where designing *Shinoharesque* facades might seem, some would say, as rather frivolous?

In *L'Esprit Nouveau*, Le Corbusier talked about the need for a new architecture and – aware of the gravity of the housing situation then facing the world – made the radical proposition: 'architecture or revolution'. He meant that either we change architecture and make our built environment more liveable, especially for the millions of workers then living in poor conditions, or a revolution would provide the transformation instead. Le Corbusier famously advocated that a house should be 'a machine for living in', stripping architecture back to its core functional duties of providing warmth, water and sanitary facilities; in effect, achieving a level of domestic comfort for the masses that until then had been limited to the privileged few.

Needless to say, Le Corbusier's own architecture rarely matched his rhetoric. Yet his call for a new architecture was answered after the Second World War by the greatest architectural transformation in the history of the world through which the living conditions of millions were dramatically improved. A comfortable

2.4 Installation by Point Supreme at *Face, Pool, Two Towers and Ruin* exhibition at Haszkovó Housing Estate, 2019.

2.5 Installation by Paradigma Ariadné, *The Fourth Ruin* at *Face, Pool, Two Towers and Ruin* exhibition at Haszkovó Housing Estate, 2019.

2.6 Works by Adam Nathaniel Furman (left) and MNPL Workshop (right) at *12 Walls* exhibition on contemporary ornamentation, 2018.

2.7 Works by Paradigma Ariadné (left) and Enorme Studio (right) at *12 Walls* exhibition on contemporary ornamentation, 2018.

home was now something that everyone could reasonably expect. However, the costs of achieving this soon became apparent in the infinite sea of housing estates that sprung up in cities across the world, and later in the environmental implications of running those buildings which had been conceived at a time when energy was assumed to be cheap and plentiful forever.

The irony of our present age is that we face a situation almost exactly the reverse of the one faced by Le Corbusier a hundred years ago. The goal isn't to create or increase the comfort provided by buildings – we've long known how to create comfortable buildings, after all. Our 'radical' goal today is to sustain the levels of comfort that modern architecture was able to make available to the masses in the face of a climate emergency to which the same movement has been a significant contributor.

Modern architecture was seen by many of its adherents as an endpoint: the rational outcome of the application of a set of pre-ordained architecture principles applied to the social and urban circumstances of the time. The image it presented was of the world transformed. Consciously or otherwise, it acted as a distraction from changes that were taking place in the world – socially and environmentally – to which it itself was contributing. Today, the goal of architecture is to find ways to reflect and accommodate those changes, and, in the case of the environment, mitigate or maybe even reverse them. Architecture's potential has never before been so important, and today we arguably stand at a juncture as seismic as the one that Le Corbusier did a hundred years ago.

As for our own work, I cannot say that at Paradigma Ariadné we design spaces with the idea in mind that they will be the last joys of a world afflicted by climate catastrophe. But I do believe that the plurality present in contemporary

2.8 Case study based on the style of the modernist Hungarian architect, György Kővári, 2020.

2.9 The St Bartholomew Hut was an installation at the Concentrico Festival at Logroño, 2021.

architecture, and the fact that an emerging generation is aiming to find ways to enrich architecture through surfaces, forms and spatial connections, will indeed play an important part. And in addition to designing, we see our role in fostering this culture of pluralism as convenors and curators, whether through the *12 Walls* exhibition, or the *Face, Pool, Two Towers and Ruin* exhibition, or the 'Pomostroika' conference, or through other diverse forms of media.

Even though the above conclusion may appear bitter-sweet, it is important to highlight that the task itself is inspirational. A lot will depend on whether we are able to build a bridge over the pessimism of a hopefully short and temporary period, drawing on the inspiration taken from the past, and in particular on the enthusiasm and alternative directions and outlooks sparked by postmodern architecture. It is worth taking a step backward if we'll then be able to take two steps forward.

2.10　Artist studio in rural Hungary, 2020.

2.11　Collection of elements of ornamentation to decorate a
formerly secessionist villa in Budapest, 2019.

3.1   Detail of *Refuge for Resurgence* which was created for the
17th International Architecture Exhibition of the Venice Architecture
Biennale (22 May – 21 November 2021). Illustration, Nicola Ferrao.

3

FROM CAUTIONARY TALES TO STORIES OF ACTIVE HOPE

THE MORE-THAN-HUMAN WORK OF SUPERFLUX

Anab Jain and Jon Ardern

A decade or so ago, design was lauded as something that innovated new things into the world. That it could become a critical strategy to choreograph and activate latent relations and emergent temporalities was still unknown, or untested.

In this space of possibility, we established Superflux in 2009. It took determination and commitment for a small adaptive practice to encourage clients, partners and institutions – at different scales and sectors – to believe in the transformative power of design-led foresight as a tool for strategic thinking and decision-making; or in other words, to place their trust in imagination.

This chapter brings together three works that embody our approach and concerns, taking the form of visceral experiences that lead to pertinent strategies for understanding both the present and the future. Together, these works point to the more-than-human perspectives that are vital to reimagining our relationship with the world and with each other.

An early ambition of the studio was to advance critical reflection on artificial intelligence technologies. One of the works that reflected this was *Drone Aviary* (2015), an investigation into drone technology's social, political and cultural potential within civic space, which constituted a foreboding cautionary tale. The short film considered the unintended consequences of increasingly sentient technologies – which we understood as a new kind of networked colonialism.

Projects such as *Drone Aviary* helped us sharpen our creative and critical focus as well as master the art of bringing high-fidelity plural futures to life.

3.2 and 3.3
Photographs of
schoolchildren
experiencing *Refuge
for Resurgence* which
was shown in the
Our Time on Earth
exhibition held at
the Barbican Centre,
London (5 May –
29 August 2022).

Enlisting storytelling foresight and material artefacts as allies, we pursued and exposed potentialities often hidden from public view.

The sharp pivot to climate-focused work came with the arrival of our son. Painfully aware of the world he was inheriting, but not wanting to feed this fear, we considered what could be possible. This became *Mitigation of Shock* (2016) – a future apartment situated in the context of climate change and its consequences on food security which people could step inside and directly experience for themselves what the restrictions of this future might feel like. Instead of leaving visitors scared by and unprepared for the challenges of this world, we shared methods and tools for not only surviving, but thriving there, demonstrating the need for transformative adaptation via tangible, actionable positivity.

Energised by this pivot, we have continued to explore our responsibility to the world and how we might develop more-than-human perspectives – as participants in, rather than masters of, nature. This led directly to two major recent works, which we present here: *Refuge for Resurgence*, a multi-species banquet; and *Invocation for Hope*, a resurgent forest born from the ashes of human destruction.[1] *Refuge for Resurgence* and *Invocation for Hope* do not advance a single viewpoint; they do not endeavour to explain, teach or warn. Instead, these open works support a plurality of potentials through a mythopoetic lens.

First presented at Biennale Architettura, La Biennale di Venezia, 2021, curated by Hashim Sarkis under the title 'How Will We Live Together?', *Refuge for Resurgence* is a multi-species banquet with a fox, rat, wasp, pigeon, cow, human adults and child, wild boar, snake, beaver, wolf, raven and mushroom. The scene lays bare a conversation between the paralysis of fear and the audacity of hope.

REFUGE FOR RESURGENCE

Working together to carve a new world out of the smouldering remains of the old. Working together to forge enduring forms of sharing and survival. Working together to revive this land, this land, once a place of order and control.

A place where all species, all forms of life, were once forced to submit to an alien law. A law that dictated what could live and where. A law labelling anything that did not obey its monolithic order 'weed', 'pest' or 'vermin'.

A law that for a time felt relentless, unending, unstoppable; until the planet rebelled and threw its house of cards to the wind. Now, in the ruins of that old world, those weeds, pests and vermin have risen, and reclaimed their rightful place at the table of planetary ecology.

Their rightful place in a new home. A home built on humility, resourcefulness and imagination. A home strong enough to weather the storm, to rise from the flood, to endure the heat.

3.4, 3.5 and 3.6
Invocation for Hope, which was exhibited
at the Museum for Applied Arts, Vienna
(28 May – 3 October 2021).

WE
ARE
OF
THIS
EARTH

3.7 and 3.8
Superflux, *A More
Than Human
Manifesto*, 2021.

Here sit a fox, rat, wasp, pigeon, cow, human adults and child, wild boar, snake, beaver, wolf, raven and mushroom. More than the mythologising of their experiences, they gather in a shared hope for our more than human future.

A hope in the resurgence of life stretched thin around this rock, painting its surface blue and green as it spins wildly in the vast blackness.

Invocation for Hope was an immersive installation in the central hall of the Museum of Applied Arts (MAK) in Vienna, created for the Vienna Biennale 2021. Designed as a living, resurgent forest, its scale and sensory experience invokes hope for a better world in the face of climate change. Accompanied by an original soundscape from Cosmo Sheldrake, visitors walked through a grid of 400 burnt pines destroyed by a recent wildfire. Moving through skeletal remains of fire-blackened trees towards the centre, death restores fertility, making way for new life – green shoots of hope.

INVOCATION FOR HOPE

The forest appears quiet. Waiting for us to listen.

Wander up the ramp. Tread carefully along the path, meander past the skeletal remains of black pine. Row after row, arranged in a perfect, orderly grid, their blackened bodies remain stubbornly standing in the damaged soil. Pause a moment. Examine the dark, uneven surfaces of the

OUR FATES ARE MORE INTERWOVEN THAN OUR PREDECESSORS KNEW

decomposing bark that still holds onto its slender host. A stark reminder of that luminous flame that swept their bare skins, extinguishing their dreams of canopying under the white sun.

Millennia of communal bonds broken by human greed in just a few hundred years. Whole ecologies disturbed by capitalism and war destroying life sustaining worlds – taking human and non-human alike.

If you lend your ear to the grid, you might hear the echoes of that calamitous terraforming in the hollow landscape.

The traces of this destruction persist in the grey rocks littered across the land. How do we move forward in this shattered landscape?

Hold onto this predicament and continue the journey to the end, and you may hear whispers of a sprightly frond, unfurling in the mythic shadows of burnt black pine. The enticing poem of a resurgent forest rising from the skeletal remains, gracefully returning fertility to the earth.

In the heart of the dead forest, a glimpse of an interdependent, tentacular flourishing, a glimpse of hope. Come along, with abandon, and embrace this spirited renewal in, and amongst, damaged ruins.

Dance with wild grasses amid adolescent trees. A spell-binding dawn chorus calling out across the midsummer morning. If you gaze into the glistening pool, what awaits? A hope for a renewal of our bonds.

STRIPPING AN
ECOSYSTEM
FOR OUR 'NEEDS'
MUST BECOME AS
ABERRANT TO US AS
CUTTING A PIECE OF
YOUR FLESH OFF
TO FEED YOURSELF.

3.9 and 3.10
Superflux, *A More
Than Human
Manifesto*, 2021.

A hope for new, collaborative world-making. Worlds where humans and non-humans carve and shape their destinies together.

An ecology of refugee species in reflection, taking strength in each other. Taking courage in the mere fact that they are not alone, that as long as there is life there is hope. Is this you? Are you them?

Welcome to our Forest.

By reframing humans in direct interdependence with other species, *Refuge for Resurgence* and *Invocation for Hope* foreground our role as participants in a larger ecology, rather than the masters of nature.

Our earlier 'cautionary tales' tackling technology and social unrest had given us the tools to address lived experience from a place of criticality and compassion. While the past few years have felt like living inside a big cautionary tale, we feel the urgency to give voice and form to imagined futures that generate active hope. In creating worlds from a more-than-human perspective as we have in these two works, we believe we can better understand our ecological, economic and emotional entanglement with all species on the planet.

These works and the ideas that drove them led us to create *A More Than Human Manifesto,* which we conceived as a challenge to long-standing histories of human exploitation and extraction. Drawing from and developing ideas explored in our work, this manifesto of intent is, quite simply, our reworking of the order of things.

WE'RE CALLING TIME ON HUMAN EXCEPTIONALISM

A MORE THAN HUMAN MANIFESTO

We are more than human. We know where we are.

Our actions have caused disastrous imbalances. The Earth's climate system is in peril: animal populations destroyed, soil degraded. People alive today will witness the extinction of thousands, if not millions, of species.

But this isn't just an abstract tragedy happening to other lifeforms. Our fates, it turns out, are more interwoven than our predecessors knew. Without our kin – butterflies, birds, bees, lichen – humanity cannot survive on earth.

That's why we're calling time on human exceptionalism. It's not working for the planet. It's not working for humanity. We believe that humankind needs to think beyond itself.

We need to remember that we are not just on this Earth: we are of this Earth. The interdependence is real: humanity as ecology, ecology as humanity. Both the head and the heart demand this mental leap, this act of surrender.

The awe of small things helps: the morning bird song; the smell of rain; the winter sunset. We need to cultivate a reverence for the beauty and embodied intelligence of our ecosystem. We need to feel that its intelligence may be greater than ours.

No more treating nature as a resource for extraction, exploitation and consumption. There is no nourishment here. Instead, we must foster mutual admiration and respect.

This more-than-human spirit will encourage us to forge new relationships with the species we share our planet with. Stripping an ecosystem for our 'needs' must become as aberrant to us as cutting a piece of your flesh off to feed yourself.

For those schooled in a dichotomy between 'humanity' and 'nature', we will need to change how we think. This will be hard. We will need a renewal of our beliefs, of what we value or think of as 'good'. New taboos, too. We will rediscover old stories, stories that, though muted by the norms of an extractive capitalism, have never gone away.

But where there is life, hope remains. We can pair incredible power with humility and care, foresight with stewardship. Real change – more-than-human change – is possible.

We need to move. Here's how:

Move from fixing to caring
Let's move away from the techno-deterministic pull of the language around 'fixing'. When we foreground the idea of care, it inherently embodies ideas of fixing, building, making and everything necessary to take care of that particular thing, person, tree, insect, bird, animal, us, them, everyone.

Move from planning to gardening
Modernism's most spectacular failures have happened when a belief in top-down planning crashes into the messy complexities of life. We should swap set squares for gardening gloves: we need to nurture and grow, adapt to rather than impose on.

Move from systems to assemblages, from knots to nodes
Acknowledging the entanglements without the desire to have the 'full overview', keeps us open to surprising possibilities. And it reflects the deeply entangled co-evolution of humans and non-humans – think wolves, men and dogs, or the soil as a living organism.

Move from innovation to resurgence

After a forest fire, seedlings sprout in the ashes, and, with time, another forest may grow up in the burn. The regrowing forest is an example of what we are calling resurgence. Whereas 'innovation' fixates on the new and the different, resurgence forges assemblages of multispecies liveability in the midst of disturbance.

Move from independence to interdependence

We value and celebrate independence, from the first steps a baby takes to the geopolitical decisions we make. What if, instead of independence, instead of constantly valuing individual success, we celebrate our interdependence with each other and all species?

Move from extinction to precarity

Rather than retreat from the anxiety of a singular, apocalyptic endpoint such as extinction, could we instead consider the possibility of precarious flourishing?

Drawing from *Refuge for Resurgence* and *Invocation for Hope* in particular, *A More Than Human Manifesto* expands upon the important role that mythology and storytelling hold as tools to navigate climate change. It proposes a larger shift in creative practices, making them less extractive, less destructive, in favour of a vocabulary which is more supportive of our planet's ecosystem, moving from 'fixing' to 'caring', from 'planning' to 'gardening'.

All of our work starts by acknowledging the fact that the future is not a fixed destination, but a constantly shifting and unfolding space of diverse potential. Central to reaching this potential is understanding that every individual experiences their world differently, based on their personal, geographic, social, and economic standing in the world. Because of this, planning for possible futures must be a diverse and inclusive process, rather than a monolithic and presumptive one. There are always multiple histories, presents, and futures – as the projects illustrated in this chapter make manifest.

Based on this position, our work aims to create futures that feel real and relatable, and give a sense of 'everydayness' and intimacy alongside the 'extraordinary' and uncertain. By creating concrete experiences from the future, we want to transform decision-making today, showing how everyone – from individuals and communities to cities, governments and corporations – can adapt to radical change, and grow and flourish in this uncertain world.

SITES

4

ATEMPORAL WISDOMS

RE-LEARNING ARCHITECTURE
IN THE RURAL CONTEXT

Xu Tiantian

Many of the environmental and social challenges that a developing country confronts are concerned with disparate growth between urban and rural regions. As the labour force migrates to urban centres, the population in rural villages diminishes, often causing economic decline. In the rural context, architecture has never been a stand-alone entity, but is intimately connected to its natural environment, local history and culture, people and community, and, in most situations, it continues to be instrumental to providing solutions and possibilities for our current issues and challenges.

This chapter explores several projects by my practice, DnA_Design and Architecture, from our eight years working in Songyang County of the Zhejiang province. These projects illustrate our approaches to working with local people, materials and contexts, and, more broadly, point to architecture's role in connecting the social, economic and material in ways that can help bring about the revitalisation of rural communities.

NATURE

4.1   Qiu Ying (1494–1552), Detail of *The Garden for Solitary Enjoyment*, 1515–52. Handscroll, painting, ink and slight colour on silk, 28 × 518.5 cm (11 × 204 ⅛ in); overall: 32 × 1290.2 cm (12 ⅝ × 507 ¹⁵⁄₁₆ in).

Traditional Chinese agrarian culture, like many others, embodies a fundamental human connection to Mother Nature, which has influenced the local way of life for centuries and inspired and shaped its architecture in ways that are sustainable over time.

The use of natural materials in vernacular buildings aligns with ancient Chinese philosophy which sees man and nature existing in harmony as one. Hence, local villagers have always drawn from materials in their immediate

4.2   Bamboo Theatre,
Hengkeng Village,
Songyang, Zhejiang,
China, 2015.

environment and continue to draw on the wisdom of ancient techniques to this day. When it comes to the process of rejuvenating, the countryside, natural materials such as timber, earth, stone and bamboo, can play critical roles, not simply in a practical sense, but in the way their cultural significance fosters a sense of local identity.

In 2015, local villagers in Hengkeng Village, which is surrounded by mountains covered with bamboo forests, built a Bamboo Theatre with a light structure using local natural resources (fig.4.2). Bamboo, a typical and abundant plant of this region, is easily used as a building material, and here, the bamboo structure maintained the open space of its natural environment. Every two years, the dead bamboos are removed, and new ones join the existing structure, making it a metabolic architecture.

A painting by the Ming Dynasty painter, Qiu Ying (1494–1552), *The Garden for Solitary Enjoyment*, portrays a similar scene, depicting Sima Guang, a literato and official historian, sitting at ease in a bamboo structure (fig.4.1). Although the painting visualises Sima Guang's personal estate, the image conveys the timeless philosophy about man living in harmony with Mother Nature. The iconography of the literato in the bamboo forest has been portrayed in art and literature throughout ancient Chinese history, forming a cultural heritage that we are continuing to learn from in the contemporary world.

INFRASTRUCTURE

In rural areas, infrastructure often plays a dual role: fulfilling a practical function, for example, in transport and logistics, but also providing shelter that brings together everyday rural activities in nature. In the mountainous junctions between Zhejiang and Fujian provinces, bridges serve as cultural icons and public buildings for local communities, as much as their more familiar role as objects of infrastructure. In particular, a roof-topped bridge, constructed to protect its wooden frame, provides pedestrians with shelter from sun and rain, and also serves as a meeting place and centre for community events.

This type of bridge inspired our renovation of the abandoned Shimen Bridge in Songyang County (fig.4.3), completed in 2017. With a new covered timber canopy, this formerly unsafe structure was converted into a pedestrian bridge reconnecting two villages across the river.

Like the traditional Lounge Bridge, which functions as a meeting point for the local community, the new Shimen Bridge became a shared multi-functional public space and viewing platform, looking out over the adjacent one-thousand-year-old ancient dam (fig.4.4).

In ancient times, the two villages, now located on different sides of the river, used to be one, and were subsequently separated due to heavy flooding. The

4.3   Shimen Bridge, Songyang, Zhejiang, China, 2017.

4.4   Shimen Bridge, Songyang, Zhejiang, China, 2017.

preservation of the former Shimen Bridge is, therefore, symbolic in uniting the villages once again, recycling an abandoned infrastructure, and applying valuable local resources to help restore local history and identity.

DWELLING

With the rural economy and population in decline, issues around housing and dwelling in rural regions are often contrary to those facing urban centres. The challenges confronted in addressing rural dwelling are not only about how to preserve vacant traditional houses, but, more importantly, how to create innovative social and economic frameworks that will increase both population growth and village revenue by stimulating new interactions between the urban and the rural.

In the case of Shangtian Village in Songyang County, whose history traces as far back as 600 years ago, the population had declined to such an extent that it was considered a 'hollowed village'. To transform such a place, it was vital to reach a common agreement with the remaining local community, before renovating and converting the vacant houses into shared 'home-stay businesses' owned by the village community.

4.5   Shangtian Village Housing, Songyang, Zhejiang, 2019.

The starting point for architectural design of such a project is to respect the village's history and preserve its original fabric by using traditional techniques and craftsmanship, while offering an alternative living – in both senses of the

4.6   Shangtian Village Co-op Housing, Songyang, Zhejiang, 2019.

word – for residents (fig.4.5). This meant establishing a hybrid, collective, rural economy to protect ownership and the village's potential economic value against exploitation and inequity from urban investments. Through this collective process, villagers' properties became local assets, making them shareholders in the new village economy, and at the same time creating opportunities for employment at the newly created businesses (fig.4.6). With such a reformed and diversified rural economy, many young villagers have returned to the village.

The Shangtian Village Transformation, as the project was known, shows the possibilities of developing a hybrid economic system which, in turn, helps bring about a new social structure, responding to the needs of villagers not only as a collective, but also as individuals who might otherwise be left behind in the market economy.

AGRICULTURAL PRODUCTION

With hundreds of years of history, and often comprising large clans, each village in Songyang County prides itself on the legacy built up by generations of its inhabitants, which provides an inspiring, but often overlooked, social material and resource.

To help release this resource, we have developed an approach we call 'Architectural Acupuncture' – a systematic and sustainable strategy to address a variety of rural issues. 'Architectural Acupuncture' is an approach of minimal intervention, where we develop complex and multi-dimensional programmes for each location, responding to its unique cultural, economic and historical context. It operates less as a solution or cure than as a spur for villages to reimagine and reinvent themselves. The following case study, in addition to those discussed already, offers a good example of the approach.

In Songyang County, the villages share similar agricultural economies. Each village, however, prides itself on its unique local products, which can be both an intangible cultural heritage and an economic resource. This led to the creation of a new programme for the tofu factory in Caizhai Village, which was tailored to the uniqueness of village agricultural production.

While aiming to improve the quality of the product and ensuring a healthy local food system, the factory also showcases traditional production methods and processes, providing a cultural experience allied to an educational workshop, as well as functioning as a village centre during seasons of non-production

4.7   Tofu factory,
Caizhai Village,
Dadongba Town,
Songyang, Zhejiang,
China, 2018.

(fig.4.7). By engaging individual family workshops as shareholders, the factory becomes an entity in the village's developing collective economy.

New factories, tailored for production and public education, increased the village's income and regional circulation. At the same time, by restoring local pride within the community, there are now more incentives for young villagers to return home. Furthermore, the educational aspect of the factories has helped to inspire a more ecological approach to agriculture, which in turn leads to higher quality raw material for production.

The integration of agricultural production, culture and educational programmes, village public space and collective co-operation has transformed the typology of the village factory into a new social structure. Architecture in rural areas often requires multi-functional, more adaptive, resilient and efficient approaches to achieve cultural, social and economic sustainability. 'Architectural Acupuncture' has played an important role in achieving this.

INDUSTRIAL HERITAGE

Besides agricultural production, rural regions have retained a significant amount of local industries, whose history stretches from a few decades to over a thousand years. The resulting local collective memories continue to shape regional characteristics.

Today, re-using and adapting existing spatial resources is regarded around the world as essential to sustainable development. For rural regions, this

presents an important new opportunity, prompting an urgent and necessary re-evaluation of local resources and re-discovery of local value. These demands, in turn, challenge architects to expand their perspectives in identifying issues and initiating collaborations.

In Jinyun County, the local landscape has been shaped by thousands of years of manual mining of natural stone, with over 3,000 abandoned small-scale quarries. Today, these abandoned sites can become valuable local resources for cultural and social activities and ecological improvements, offering new economic potential for the rural population (fig.4.8).

By re-using the abandoned quarries as new public cultural facilities, our project reduces the requirement for new buildings and their environmental impact. But this is only part of the story. Ruins left behind from exploitation of the land are now transformed into a cultural stage that brings new perspectives to village communities in the region, both ecologically and economically. By transforming an industrial wasteland into a symbol of hope in the rural hinterland, the quarry also revives a piece of collective memory that reconnects the local community with its long history (fig.4.9).

The phrase, 'rural is global', epitomises our belief in the power of systematic, local-scale interventions to offer strategic and sustainable solutions with an impact that extends far beyond. With many agrarian societies practising a way of life based on the notion of balancing harmony between man and nature, the rural continues to be a timeless model from which contemporary architects can draw wisdom.

4.8 Quarry 8, Jinyun County, Zhejiang, China, 2022.

Compared to the often large-scale developments or iconic landmark buildings that have played a defining role in China's urbanisation process, the impacts of architecture targeting rural issues – though proven to be much more sustainable for small-scale local demands – may appear by definition to be limited to those local areas. However, by being centred on the art of achieving a fine balance between man and nature, the strategies for rural revitalisation which we have learned and adopted in Songyang County offer transformative possibilities for arresting imminent environmental disasters and socio-economic decline.

4.9　Quarry 9, Jinyun County, Zhejiang, China, 2022.

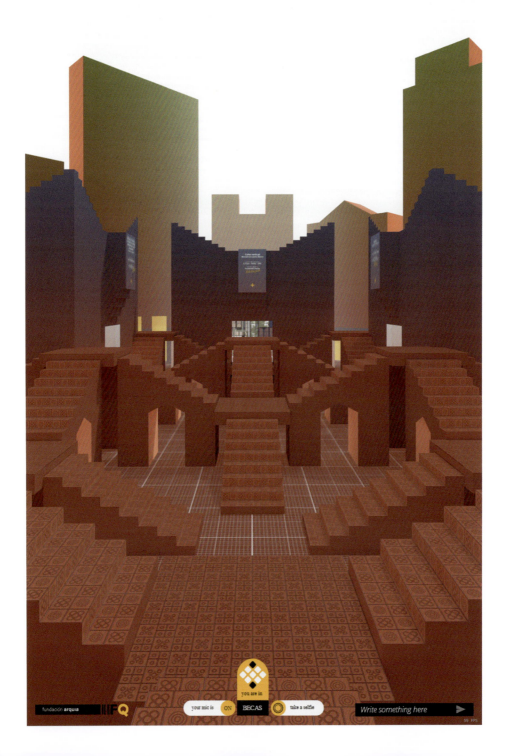

5

TOWARDS A LIQUID ARCHITECTURE

Gonzalo Herrero Delicado

In 1867, Karl Marx published *Das Kapital*. In this seminal work, he described technology as a means to reveal the active relation of man to nature, a direct process of the production of his life. According to Marx, technology can redefine the production process of social relations, and the mental conceptions that flow from those relations.

Das Kapital was followed in 1884 by *Economic and Philosophic Manuscripts* in which Marx defined the concept of estranged or 'alienated' labour. This alienation was categorised into four types: alienation from nature, from other people, from our work, and from ourselves. These four forms of alienation were intrinsically connected to the impact of the new technologies brought about by the Industrial Revolution. These technologies radically transformed economies that had been based on agriculture and handicrafts into economies based on large-scale industry, mechanised manufacturing and the factory system.

In 2021, the global augmented reality (AR), virtual reality (VR) and mixed reality (MR) markets reached $28 billion, and it is widely expected that these virtual technology markets will increase in size by ten-fold within the decade. These technologies, along with other information and communication technologies that comprise the so-called Fourth Industrial Revolution, will have a drastic impact on the ways we interact with the world around us, leading to the radical transformation not only of economies, but of social interaction and spatial experience. As happened in previous industrial revolutions, this new one comes with an even higher risk of 'alienation', and it is crucial to question the impact and design challenges that these technologies – widely heralded under the banner of the metaverse – will present to the environment, our connection to other beings – humans and non-humans – and our own bodies.

The term 'metaverse' was coined by Neal Stephenson in the 1992 science fiction novel *Snow Crash*. Stephenson imagined the metaverse as a successor to the internet, taking the form of a virtual reality-based urban environment resembling a multiplayer online game and populated by user-controlled avatars. The virtual real estate is owned by a fictional corporation and is available to be bought and buildings developed thereupon. It is an uncannily prescient formulation that mirrors many aspects of what we understand as the metaverse today – a space designed for work and social life where value can be speculated.

For over a decade, major technology companies including Apple, Google, Meta, Microsoft, Epic and Niantic have been developing the technologies that will shape the future of the metaverse, designing its virtual platforms and developing the hardware required to access them. In this context, a critical examination of the design of the social and spatial contexts of the metaverse will be key to revealing its challenges and full potential. It is fundamental that architects and other spatial practitioners are involved in these contexts' inception and definition.

Although the metaverse might feel far away from traditional concepts of architecture and urbanism, it is important to understand that its spatial qualities and user experience are very similar to those of cities. Instead of being built with bricks and mortar, the metaverse is made of pixels following Cartesian rules that define how they are designed and navigated. In addition,

5.2   Facebook's test of its new Horizon Workrooms remote-working app for its virtual reality Oculus Quest 2 headsets is shown in this press image run in a story by Reuters (and others) on 19 August 2021. www.reuters.com/ technology/facebook-launches-vr-remote-work-app-calling-it-step-metaverse-2021-08-19/.

existing technologies, including VR headsets and full-body haptic suits, will soon allow multi-sensorial experiences that resemble what we can feel in the physical world.

The way people navigate, interact and perform in these spaces requires an understanding of many of the conditions that organise and rule our cities today. As happens in the physical world, issues such as abuse, racism and sexism are already appearing in a number of these 'metaverse' spaces. Tackling this does not mean replicating the structures, systems and regulations of the physical world, but instead embracing decentralised autonomous organisations (DAOs), which have the potential to build a future democratic metaverse, empowering people to decide themselves how the metaverse is regulated and to take control of their own data.

In terms of the experience they offer, communicating emotions and enhancing other senses beyond sight and hearing are some of the main challenges that these digital platforms face today, and they will require years or even decades of development to create a more accurate physical experience. Yet, designing spaces that allow for both normative and spontaneous forms of communication and exchange is already feasible. We might not need benches to sit and have a conversation with other avatars, but we need virtual spaces that incite open discussions or encourage intimate conversations, as it would happen respectively in a public square or a corner of a room.

Virtual spaces are increasingly in demand, particularly from younger generations. According to a recent survey of over 5,000 metaverse gamers of the top three games – *Minecraft*, *Fortnite* and *Roblox* – the largest group of users are below the age of 20.[1] The survey also identified that the main reasons why young people are using these online spaces are, first, to connect with other people and, second, to escape reality. Yet, aside from the examples cited above, many of the social contexts in the metaverse are those dedicated to work, such as the spaces offered by Horizon Workrooms or Meeting VR. These platforms often replicate traditional settings, such as the office or a meeting space based on people sitting around a table, betraying a worrying lack of imagination which, if unchanged, will only further exacerbate alienation from one another.

To capitalise on the imaginative potential of a weightless architecture with endless possibilities for the design of alternative social and spatial contexts requires a fundamental shift in architectural thinking. The sociologist and philosopher Zygmunt Bauman coined the concept of 'liquid modernity' as a metaphor to describe the condition of constant mobility and change in relationships, identities and global economics within contemporary society. The metaverse takes things even further: a space that exists in a state of constant redefinition in response to constant contextual changes. Following Bauman, to be able to structure and make sense of the metaverse we need a 'liquid architecture' – one that is attuned to the challenges and potentials of the metaverse.

But how do we bring this liquid architecture into being? Over the last decades, many architects have imagined the possibilities of building in the virtual world, but have often failed by understanding this space as a mere translation of the spaces of the physical world. Despite the limitations of the available technologies at the time, perhaps one of the more successful and remarkable early attempts was the *Virtual Guggenheim Museum* (1999) by Asymptote Architecture: a dynamic, three-dimensional virtual space, whose spiralling form was loosely inspired by Frank Lloyd Wright's architecture for the Guggenheim Museum in New York. Creatively referencing existing built architectures in the virtual in this way remains an important strategy that will allow for a transition and adaptation into the possibilities of this yet unknown territory for users and architects, making these spaces recognisable and easy to navigate. However, a balance needs to be struck. We are navigating towards a new form of architecture that requires a mental adaptation to, first, understand and, later, control how it is to be navigated. Yet, it is crucial that this transition evokes an imaginative and provoking future which maximises the potential of available technologies.

In 2020, I commissioned Space Popular, a practice led by Lara Lesmes and Fredrik Hellberg, to create a virtual platform to host the 7th Arquia Festival run by the Arquia Foundation. The festival is held every two years in a different city, and that year the hosting city was Barcelona. Due to the COVID-19 lockdown, the physical event had to be cancelled and instead it was proposed to organise a virtual festival. At that time, most digital events were held on platforms such as Zoom or Microsoft Teams, but instead we wanted to recreate the social dimension and lively meeting space that the festival had always been. Following this brief, Space Popular designed a virtual space hosted on the open-source platform Mozilla Hubs, which took as a starting point the architecture of the historical centre of Barcelona. The intention was that people would recognise building elements and the iconic grid that shapes the city, thereby making their experience more accessible. The result was an

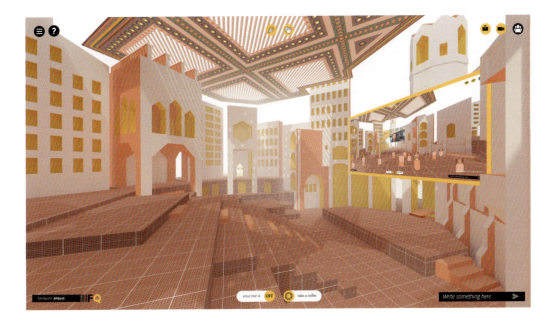

5.3 'The Arena is an amphitheatre space that takes us into another area of Barcelona: Barrio Gótico. Following the Ensanche block shape as all other rooms, the Arena is organised along the diagonal axis with the stage platform fanning out from one of its corners.'
www.spacepopular.com/2020---punto-de-inflexion---vii-festival-arquia-proxima.

5.4 'In order to be able to afford having as many visitors as possible [Space Popular] designed the avatars ... to be a single plane that contains two images (back and front). Even though they are quite abstract, avatars are given basic body language such as moving their eyes, heads and bodies in response to different audio and navigation inputs.'
www.spacepopular.com/2020---punto-de-inflexion---vii-festival-arquia-proxima.

5.5   'To overcome the restrictions of 2020 the organisers and curator of Punto de Inflexión (Turning Point) VII Festival Arquia/Próxima, 2020, commissioned Space Popular to create a virtual city for the festival where lectures, debates and ceremonies could be held and new communities could form.' www.spacepopular.com/2020---punto-de-inflexion---vii-festival-arquia-proxima.

imaginative and visionary space where festival attendees hung out for hours attending talks, visiting exhibitions and chatting with others. This is a small but revealing example of the possibilities of involving spatial practitioners in the design of social and spatial contexts in the metaverse.

In 2010, architect Winy Maas, founder of MVRDV, and Philip Rosedale, founder of Linden Lab which developed and hosts *Second Life*, joined in conversation to explore the proximity of built and virtual environments, ideologies, social systems and visions of the future.[2] In the talk, they examined the initial importance of the pre-metaverse *Second Life* platform to empower people to design and control this space but also its potential to speculate with its value. For Rosedale, *Second Life* was 'an architecture of spectacular imagination that doesn't obey the rules of physics, [it is] surprisingly life-like – not a completely imaginary world – and economically motivated'. Almost a decade before the COVID-19 pandemic, Rosedale offered a tantalising glimpse of how the ways we congregate and meet face-to-face in cities would radically change in the future through to virtualisation, while also prefiguring some of its potential downsides.

The user-created platform was originally aimed at empowering people to create their own world, which led to a seemingly inevitable transactional system where people could digitally design and sell their own creations. In the early 2010s, *Second Life* experienced a mass economic growth

5.6 'Creator Jenaia Morane describes *Braided Lives* as "a multimedia, multiplatform initiative designed to bring people from around the planet together to create, collaborate, and build community." It currently features a music installation called Songs for Ukraine.' second.life/cf041922.

5.7 'Established in 2014, *Peak Lounge* has been providing a fun and relaxed place for Residents that enjoy music and dancing. Peace, love, and music is their motto! There are live DJs from all over the world playing a variety of music from different genres.' second.life/cf010422.

which also came with the possibility to acquire standardised domestic architectures. *Linden Homes* – which, via digital avatar, you could buy and make your own – were first introduced in 2010, with the second generation of New Linden Homes becoming available in 2019. Currently, the game offers different home typologies including Victorian houses, campers, log homes and houseboats. Far from the 'spectacular imagination' claimed by their creator, it has become not so different to typical, speculative, real estate products.

In the same talk, Rosedale also described the 'ecology of virtualisation' and argued that this shift towards a more virtual lifestyle would be positive for the environment, reducing carbon emissions brought about by commuting and the use of dedicated spaces for work and leisure that require heating and lighting. Today, we know that the increasing demand for information and communication technologies, including data centres, has a massive impact on the environment. By 2030, it is expected that collectively they will be responsible for around 20 per cent of global greenhouse emissions. The architecture we experience in the metaverse may be weightless but it nevertheless has a vast material impact and carbon footprint, and this must be at the forefront of any discussion among architects about the role they might play in designing the metaverse. The risk, otherwise, is further alienation from nature.

5.8 First released in April 2015, Second Life's 'Traditional suburban homes are available in several single or two-story options and are located within a convenient distance from a communal park area where you can join your friends for picnics, sports, or family activities.' https://community. secondlife.com/blogs/ entry/2528-fresh-new-linden-homes-are-here-with-new-themes-and-larger-options/.

Trying to define the metaverse today would be like trying to describe what the internet was in the 1970s. Back then, no-one knew what it would become and the communication, social interaction and knowledge exchange possibilities that it would bring. Today, the metaverse is similarly in its infancy, and it will take a few decades to unveil its full potential. What is certain is that we must find ways to avoid the alienating effects on the planet, society, and ourselves which have taken place during previous industrial revolutions. Architects have a vital role in laying the first (digital) stones towards a more optimistic and democratic future for the metaverse and the digital commons, but only if we embrace the possibilities of 'liquid architecture'.

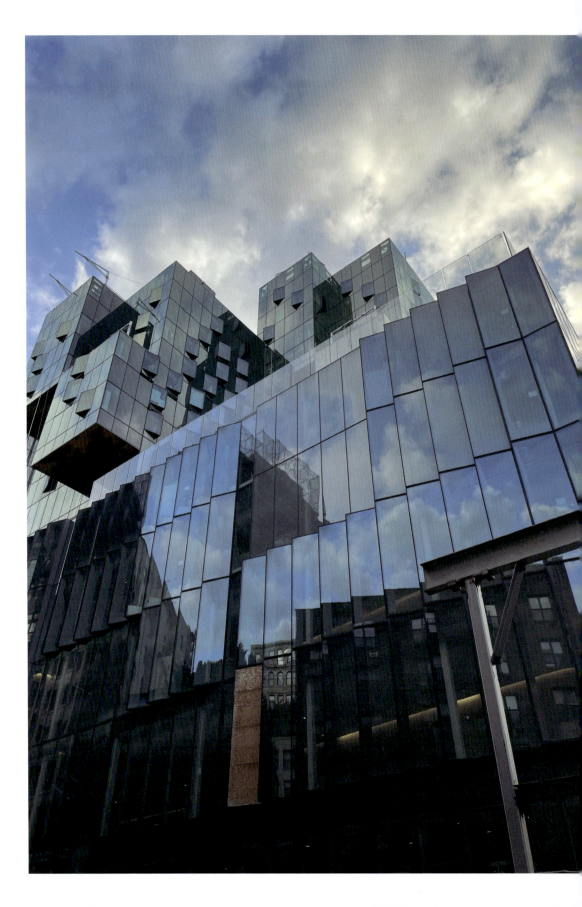

6

ANOTHER WAY OF WRITING

REIMAGINING ARCHITECTURE CRITICISM

Marianela D'Aprile

In order to move towards a way of making architecture different from the kind we see today, we need first to move towards a different way of thinking about architecture. This is, of course, easier said than done. The way that architecture is made is determined largely by specific and practical considerations: the needs of for-profit developers or private clients; building codes and regulations, the requirements of which can often only be met by using certain materials in certain configurations that can end up being environmentally damaging; value engineering – itself colours deeply the way that people who make architecture think about it. At the most basic level, architects have to make sure that a building can exist at all: that it's compliant, that it fulfils programmatic requirements, that it meets the client's budget. Only after these basic material requirements are met can architects begin to aspire to make a building that transcends the pragmatic brief and aspires to something we might see as artistry.

Despite the fact that practical questions influence much of the reasoning behind architectural decisions, a significant portion of mainstream writing about architecture – the type you might find on *Dezeen* or *ArchDaily* online, or in glossy design magazines – focuses overwhelmingly on the superficial results of these considerations, as opposed to examining the considerations themselves. Instead of treating buildings as the materialisation of a specific set of economic interests and of the practical requirements that those interests play a major role in determining, this sort of writing treats buildings as isolated art objects, the result of a set of purely aesthetic design decisions made by an architect. At its worst, it is barely writing at all, little more than the copying and pasting of press releases alongside copious images, the quality of which largely decides whether a building is deemed worthy of publication or not.

6.1 The approach suggested in this chapter does not discount formal analysis, but rather aims to incorporate it into a larger critique. Here, the older brick buildings reflected in the NYU building's facade might serve as a jumping-off point for analysing the university's role in the development of the neighbourhood, 2022.

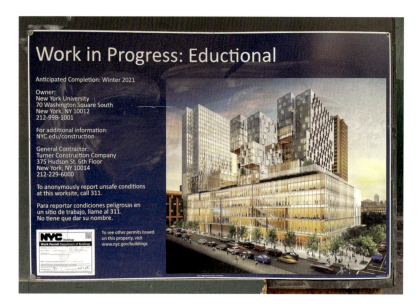

6.2 Work in Progress notices are a good clue into the social and political contexts of a project. Here, in Manhattan, a New York University development highlights the role of the urban university as a real estate speculator, 2022.

This is not the fault of the writers, rather a set of editorial policies determined by the structures and systems of the online world and the need to compete in its attention economy. For this reason, it would be easy to write off this kind of writing. Yet I focus on it here – alongside the writing that appears in the few newspapers still covering architecture seriously – not only because it is the field to which I dedicate a large portion of my time and energy, but also because it has the potential to be the clearest and farthest-reaching expression of thinking about architecture. It is a part of the constellation of artefacts that shape how architects think about what they do, but also how the general public think about what architects do. (Also in that constellation: architects' own educations, fictionalised depictions of architects and architecture, advertising, real estate development.) If we are going to change either of those ways of thinking, hopefully as a first step towards changing how buildings are made, then we have to change how we write about architecture.

This is not a new proposition. The two arguably most influential architecture critics in 20th-century America, Jane Jacobs and Ada Louise Huxtable, were to different degrees concerned with urbanism and the social effects of architecture, and their work deeply shaped the landscape of architecture writing. Today, publications such as *Failed Architecture* – which has a global audience and a broad-sweeping left political agenda – and *Urban Omnibus* – which keeps a close focus on New York City – publish writing about architecture that examines the larger systems that influence how buildings are made, who makes them, and who gets to inhabit them. In much of this

6.3 Graffiti on a downtown Brooklyn residential rendering calls out potential gentrification anxiety in the area – a clue into the project's social and political context that could be followed, 2022.

writing, the primary object of critique is not a particular building, but rather everything around it: sources of funding, extractive practices, labour policy, infrastructure, public policy. We need this sort of writing to make sense of the world, to make visible logics that might be invisible to the naked eye, and to begin to understand our place in the large, interwoven networks that make up the globalised economy and determine what our world looks like and how it works. And we also need writing that makes sense of buildings as individual phenomena within these larger networks.

There is a hunger for this sort of writing among both architects and the general public, with the second group, to my mind, representing a crucial audience for architecture writers. People spend enormous portions of their lives in buildings. They serve as shelter, yes, but they also shape civic identity and people's relationship to the place they call (or don't call) home. They crystallise economic and class relationships; they generate civic pride; they exacerbate inequality; they contribute to climate crisis. It stands to reason that people from all walks of life would be curious about the buildings that surround them and why they look the way they do. Criticism of the sort I mentioned before, which treats architecture as an isolated art object, too often makes the mistake of telling people exactly what to see when they look around. This kind of writing doesn't produce understanding but rather encourages judgement. What I'm after, instead, is architecture writing that both acknowledges buildings as interesting and worthy objects of study and, rather than telling people what to see in a building, renders visible the invisible networks around it.

The starting point for producing such writing is to understand buildings as a singular expression of those invisible networks. From there, questions can follow that elucidate exactly why a building looks and acts the way it does. How did building codes and regulations influence the choice of materials? How did zoning and planning policy shape the way the building sits on its site? Which decisions were a result of budget limitations? Because architecture is so dependent on a variety of practical considerations that involve legal, economic and political networks extending far beyond the limits of any individual building, it is a great gateway to understanding these larger forces and how they express themselves in different contexts and situations. Two apartment buildings in two cities, for example, could look wildly different due to varying programmatic or planning requirements, or they could look surprisingly similar due to cost-minimising decisions that lead architects to choose the same sorts of materials and assembly systems despite location or climate.

6.4 and 6.5
A stop work order on a residential project near Prospect Park in Brooklyn points toward permit and labour issues. A discerning critic might follow this lead in a piece that addresses the development, 2022.

I'm not proposing that this sort of writing is the end-all, be-all solution to changing how we make architecture. Rather, I want to suggest that if we are going to dedicate published space to words about buildings, then those words must elucidate something about their subject, and the world to which it belongs, in a way that appeals to people curious about the buildings that surround them, whether or not they are architects. Moving towards another architecture requires another way of writing about architecture, one that fosters understanding instead of judgement, that doesn't tell people what to see, but rather invites them to look.

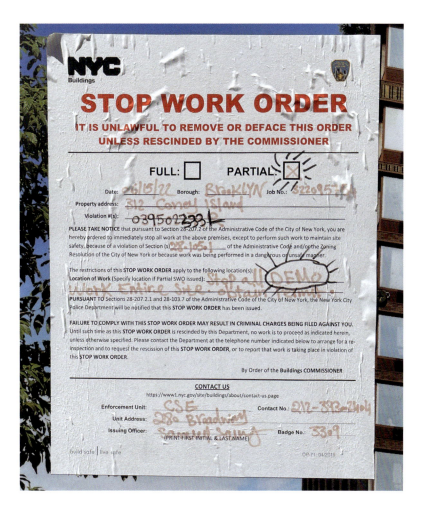

ALLIANCES

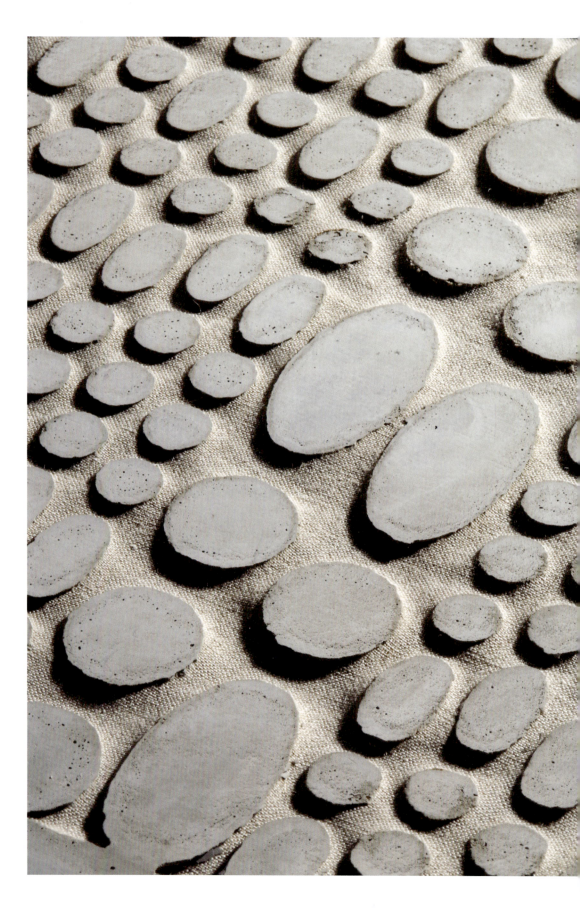

7

THE ADAPTIVE EXPERTISE OF THE COLLABORATING ARCHITECT

Ruth Morrow

In an increasingly complex and interconnected world, collaboration unlocks new alliances with new potentials. Architects have long understood collaboration when delivering buildings, but in this chapter I want to discuss how new constellations of collaborative practices can lead us towards new architectures. It draws on the experience of three material-led practices that involved a variety of human and more-than-human collaborations. Via three project case studies, I argue for an architecture of collaboration taking several forms: unlikely collaborations that bring odd or adjunct human and material collaborators together; collaborations with critical users or those people who are typically 'last on the list' of potential co-creators; slow and evolving collaborations with more-than-human organisms; and finally, digitally enabled and curated crowd collaborations that engage more minds and more hands on the development of new emerging technologies.

The first project – Tactility Factory – was driven by a collaboration with a textile designer. We came together with the singular concept 'to make hard things soft' by deploying concrete and textile technologies. The project moved beyond conceptual design and theoretical grounding, through technical innovation and resolution, to commercialisation. It required the input of a range of other experts: textile technologists, glue specialists, concrete researchers and precast concrete experts.

As the project was scaled up and commercialised, we also worked with investors, marketing experts, commercial agents and patent attorneys. Unlikely collaborations emerged that we hadn't anticipated. The patent attorney, for example, played a significant role in helping us articulate and 'own the technology', not only in the legal sense but also intellectually and emotionally. Neither of us

7.1 Linen infused concrete, Tactility Factory, Belfast, 2011.

had previous experience with intellectual property, tending to view technology as a means to an end. Even the textile designer had never thought of her processes as 'technological', despite using some 'hard-core' chemical and mechanical processes to produce her textiles. The term 'technology' is of course historically gendered and rarely assigned to the processes that women engage in.

Perhaps even more significant than the collaboration with the patent attorney was the unlikely collaboration between the materials themselves. We used standard concrete mixes and relatively common textile processes. However, those technological worlds had never previously come together in the ways we deployed them. Few would have predicted the potential of their fusion, and even fewer could have imagined that what started as a conceptual statement of 'making hard things soft' would result in the commercialisation of patented technology. The most evocative and indicative of the unpredictability of the unlikely material collaborations was the combination of linen and concrete, a collaboration between culturally diverse technologies. As a cellulosic fibre, linen is resilient in the alkali environment of concrete, and its relationship to water means that as the concrete and textiles cure in place, the linen shrinks, creating an articulated surface that would be costly to replicate by any other means of production (figs 7.1, 7.2 and 7.3).

Transplastics, the second project case study, addressed the problem of waste plastic, only seven per cent of which is currently recycled. The project aimed to design and prototype a building block using circular design principles. Central to this was bringing design thinking and user experience together in the earliest stages of material development. This was done with the aim of aligning user values to technological advancements in order to increase the likelihood of the adoption and longevity of emerging technologies. There are already existing examples of recycled plastic building blocks; however, they tend to be finished with render or other materials due to their finish and appearance. In this project we set out to design and prototype a building block that both functioned and embodied its green credentials in a manner that people could value.

The team was made up of polymer production researchers, practising architects, design researchers, a psychologist, a polymer scientist and a focus group of 'critical users', that is, people with sensory impairments. We designed the block to suit the chosen manufacturing method (rotational moulding), a relatively low cost and accessible process. In addition, the polymer scientist focused on designing recycled blends of waste plastic, establishing their mechanical properties and suitability for rotational moulding. We were particularly interested

7.2   Linen and digital stitch infused concrete, Playhouse Frieze, Derry, 2009.

7.3   Linen infused concrete in a petal design, Tactility Factory, Belfast, 2012.

in blending polymers with other waste streams such as hemp fibres, sugar cane, red mud and recycled, crushed concrete.

Early material samples and scale models were brought into workshops with people with sensory differences. The onset of the COVID-19 pandemic curtailed the number of possible interactions; however, even limited user feedback provided insights that altered the direction of the project. Some of the plastics, though visually smooth, had micro-undulations on their surfaces, due to the presence of other waste materials. This would normally be seen as a flaw in plastic manufacturing, but in this project the user groups reacted positively to the textured plastic samples, with some referring to smooth surfaces as 'claustrophobic' since they offered little to no sensory response. This insight led the project to develop more hybrid polymers that resulted in some unique material results. This critical user collaboration meant the project stepped beyond simply responding to the demands of manufacturing processes and the technical performance of the materials to develop criteria of human or *humane* performance, moving towards co-creating a social aesthetic for the waste plastic building block (figs 7.4, 7.5 and 7.6).

The third project case study is the work in the Hub for Biotechnology in the Built Environment (HBBE) at Newcastle University where, as part of a series of

7.4 Recycled plastic interlocking blocks, EPSRC Accept Project, Queen's University Belfast, 2019.

7.5 and 7.6
Tactile surfaces of recycled plastic interlocking blocks, incorporating waste streams, EPSRC Accept Project, Queen's University Belfast, 2019.

living prototypes, we are working on the application of bacterial cellulose as a facade material. Bacterial cellulose is secreted by certain types of bacteria. It is robust, biocompatible and biodegradable, and can be grown anywhere, under relatively achievable and benign conditions. Unlike other biomaterials used in traditional construction – for example, timber, bamboo or reeds – it does not require land that might otherwise be used for food production, nor does it require sunshine. Hence it can be grown in stacked assemblies, resulting in a significantly higher yield per area in comparison to other plant-based cellulose. However, we are in the very early stages of understanding the potentials and challenges of this material 'beyond the lab'. It requires us to collaborate with more-than-human organisms, without imprinting previous material relationships on these new biomaterials.

Within HBBE those who work with biomaterials, including bacterial cellulose, mycelium and algae, spend significant amounts of time observing and working with the organisms, investigating the significance of context and conditions on their behaviours. Where architects and engineers speak of building 'tolerance' into their designs to allow for material changes due to moisture and/or temperature variations, HBBE researchers aim to develop an understanding of the degree of 'growth deviation' across different conditions.

At times, though, it is difficult to avoid the default thinking of architecture – that is, applying knowledge and experience of normative materials and assembly to these new emerging materials: the bacterial cellulose prototype, for example, references timber shingle construction (figs 7.7, 7.8 and 7.9). While it's almost inevitable that the work begins from such starting points, it is important that current values, aesthetics or practices do not limit the potential for these materials.

Nevertheless, we have to acknowledge that our understanding of the materials we currently use in architecture has evolved over millennia. Humans have been crafting and constructing with wood for over 10,000 years, so we should naturally expect that it will take time to evolve sophisticated collaborations with these new living materials. We can look for ways to advance and support material development by collaborating with biodesign online and DIY communities. They already have the tools, though perhaps not at scale, and are engaged in online fora and digitally connected communities that support experimentation and open knowledge exchange.

We have begun to tap into this crowd-sourced craft expertise to ask what we can learn about emergent biotechnologies from historic craft practices. By engaging crafters to work with new biomaterials, the hope is to unearth

7.7   Bacterial cellulose shingles photographed at the time of installation, Hub for Biotechnology in the Built Environment, Newcastle University, 2021.

7.8   (detail) Bacterial cellulose shingles photographed at the time of installation, Hub for Biotechnology in the Built Environment, Newcastle University, 2021.

7.9   Bacterial cellulose shingles, photographed when dried after several weeks, Hub for Biotechnology in the Built Environment, Newcastle University, 2022.

important know-how and tacit knowledge that will inform the future development and application of these new materials. Through such digitally enabled and curated crowd collaborations with citizen scientists, DIYers and crafters, we aim to reduce the amount of time required for humans to get to know these new materials, while also helping to build an interactive and inclusive culture around biotechnology.

What does this mean for the practice of the architect? Improvisational theory gives us some insights into how we can act in these highly creative moments of collaboration and co-creation. It uses the term 'adaptive expertise' to refer to knowledge and skills that are circumstantial and contextualised within the improvised event. Like normative expertise, adaptive expertise is gained through practice and experience, but rather than being asserted in the improvisation, it is attested to in the practice *before* the improvisation. It is the preparation that allows the actor, the improvisor, the collaborator to be responsive in the context and, ultimately, adaptively expert with others.

So, to be in collaboration – with other disciplines, critical users, materials and/or non-humans – we must be skilled architects, assured of our expertise, yet able to set aside our need to assert that expertise and avoid seeking to control the outcome. In other words, we have to be able to give ourselves over to the collaboration. Collaboration often requires time to ferment, but at its most successful it takes those involved to places they can't foresee, where new outcomes and even more profound forms of collaboration emerge.

KEY COLLABORATORS

Tactility Factory: Trish Belford (textile designer), Maurice Neill (precast concrete expert), Tactility Factory Team and Board Members

Transplastics: Peter Martin, Sibele Piedade Cestari, Mark Kearns and Paul Hanna (Polymer Processing Research Centre, Queen's University Belfast); Chantelle Niblock (Architecture, Queen's University Belfast); Martin Dempster (Psychology, Queen's University Belfast); Robert Jamison (practising architect, Belfast); Guide Dogs for the Blind, Belfast Committee

HBBE Bacterial Cellulose project: Karolina Bloch, Ben Bridgens, Armand Agraviador, Mahab Aljannat, Oliver Perry

8

BUILD LONGER TABLES, NOT HIGHER WALLS

ACTION, ACTIVISM AND EQUALITY IN THE BUILT ENVIRONMENT

Alice Brownfield

We live in a time marked by global crisis: of climate, human rights, global poverty, lack of decent affordable housing, rising cost of living, physical and mental health epidemics. As architects, we must recognise our discipline's own agency within these wider societal crises and use its creativity to act radically, collaboratively and now. Central to this is working with existing fabric, adapting, densifying and retrofitting – conserving social and environmental resources.

The following text focuses specifically on equitable housing and urban design, drawing on my work as a Director of Peter Barber Architects (PBA), as trustee for Action on Empty Homes and co-chair of Part W, an action group campaigning for gender equity in the built environment, which was founded in 2018 by Zoë Berman. It argues that architects must take back the initiative in creating a more socially just and environmentally sound world.

ANOTHER ARCHITECTURE SEES HOUSING AS BASIC INFRASTRUCTURE, NOT COMMODITY

In the Austrian capital, more than 60 per cent of residents live in 440,000 social homes, about half owned directly by the municipal government and the rest by state-subsidised, not-for-profit co-operatives.

8.1   New homes by Peter Barber Architects sit nestled within the existing at the Kiln Place Estate, Camden, 2021.

The New Statesman (September 2019)[1]

Every year from 2009 to 2019 [the last survey undertaken due to COVID-19], Mercer's Quality of Living survey has named Vienna as the best place to live in the entire world.

'Quality of living city ranking (2019)', Mercer[2]

The UK is one of the largest economies in the world. Yet in England alone there are 274,000 people recorded as homeless, nearly half of whom are children.[3] We also know that, while the majority of people recorded as street homeless in the UK are male, 67 per cent of those recorded as statutorily homeless are women.[4]

It doesn't have to be this way. In the aftermath of the Second World War, when the country was effectively bankrupt, the government built over 150,000 new social rent homes a year (at the same time as founding the NHS). There was a commitment to treat housing as basic infrastructure, not a commodity. By 1977, nearly half the population lived in social housing. Since Margaret Thatcher's Housing Act 1980, however, and the failure of successive governments to address the ensuing housing crisis, this has sunk to less than eight per cent today.[5]

The COVID-19 pandemic foregrounded how the design of our homes can directly affect our physical and mental health, further highlighting the inequity that exists in access to decent affordable housing, and the importance of good design.

At PBA, our work is underpinned by the notion that housing projects are pieces of city and the belief that good design creates the potential for social action. Adopting a high-density, low/mid-rise approach prioritises streets as social spaces. Beechwood Mews, a recent project in north London, epitomises the practice's approach. On a challenging site with an initial anticipation that 35 new homes could be built, we managed to achieve 97, plus a local corner shop and a cafe, in part by reducing internal communal circulation so as to realise a much higher ratio of habitable space. As a result, of these 97 new homes, 83 have their own front door opening out onto a new, pedestrianised mews street (figs 8.2 and 8.3). In this way, careful design not only increases the quantity and quality of housing, but also pushes social life into the street. Homes of different tenures can be pepper-potted around the site, creating the opportunity for equitable and diverse communities.

8.2 Axonometric of Peter Barber Architects' Beechwood Mews, Barnet, 2020.

8.3 Completed view of Peter Barber Architects' Beechwood Mews, Barnet, 2022.

Good design can be transformational to people's lives. As architects, we have a responsibility to use design critically: creating higher quality, equitable housing, while campaigning for investment in social housing and greater rent controls.

ANOTHER ARCHITECTURE BRINGS EMPTY HOMES BACK INTO USE

A £29m project to bring more than 250 much-needed homes to Ebbw Vale has been hailed an 'exciting new development' by the local authority.

Blaenau Gwent County Borough Council[6]

Blaenau Gwent County Borough Council [of which Ebbw Vale is the largest town] is currently investigating the presence of approximately 800 empty properties within the Borough.

Blaenau Gwent County Borough Council[7]

Even though there are approximately 274,000 homeless in England, there are 653,000 empty homes.[8] Empty homes exist both in areas of chronic under-investment – typically where large industry has ceased to exist – and in the centre of major cities such as London where homes have become investment vehicles and pension funds, and left vacant.

The campaigning organisation, Action on Empty Homes (AEH), is leading the way in advocating for empty homes to be brought back into use for those in housing need. Supported by ACAN (Architects' Climate Action Network), AEH's recent Call to Action highlights the opportunity that empty homes provide to kickstart a mass retrofit programme: testing supply chains, logistics and community-led action. This is vital if we are going to reduce the built environment's carbon footprint.

We must stop building new homes where there are already significant numbers of empty homes that can be brought back into sustainable use. Instead, we must advocate for significant investment in areas that have been historically overlooked, helping to bring back employment, amenities and infrastructure.

ANOTHER ARCHITECTURE AVOIDS UNNECESSARY DEMOLITION, PRIORITISING REUSE AND ADAPTATION

Post war estates across the country are ripe for redevelopment, we will sweep away planning blockages and take new steps to reduce political and reputational risk for project investors and developers . . . together we can tear down everything that stands in our way.

David Cameron, 2016[9]

[Kiln Place Estate] is more than a sum of its many parts – the logic of all the new homes working in synthesis with the smaller interventions to bring the more monolithic slab blocks down to the scale of the street, and gently working the estate into its surroundings . . . Until the state takes its responsibilities of care seriously, until it recognises housing as a human right, Kiln Place stands as proof that so much can be done through many small gestures.

Max L. Zarzycki, *The Architectural Review*, 2021[10]

In London, the ongoing demolition of social housing estates and their replacement by predominantly market sale housing is resulting in the net loss of social rent homes, social infrastructure and substantial amounts of embodied carbon.

Our first approach at PBA is to try to avoid demolition wherever possible. Our work with residents and officers at Kiln Place Estate in Camden – a 1970s estate arranged across four- to five-storey slab blocks – provides 15 new homes, including seven for social rent in perpetuity, alongside a series of significant wider estate improvements (figs 8.1 and 8.4). For us, it serves as a modest yet potentially transformative example of how we can densify our towns and cities while improving where people live physically, socially and environmentally.

Scaling up these ideas, our proposal for the nearby Wendling Estate would provide over 150 new homes among the existing 240. These additions require the reconfiguration of just twelve existing homes and, fundamentally, avoid wholesale estate demolition (fig.8.5). Even if we build new Passivhaus homes, if buildings have been demolished to facilitate development, it takes

8.4 Existing site plan and Peter Barber Architects' proposed site plan for the Kiln Place Estate, Camden, 2021.

8.5 Axonometric of Peter Barber Architects' proposal for the Wendling Estate, Camden.

decades in use to recoup the lost carbon.[11] We must continue to call on central government to equalise, or even reverse, the VAT rates on refurbishment and new-build.

ANOTHER ARCHITECTURE MEANS EQUITABLE DESIGN

Part W campaigns for gender equity both in the design of the built environment and within its professions. Gender discrimination in the built environment operates at a range of scales and in ways that are not always apparent. To take just one example, women undertake 75 per cent of the world's unpaid care work.[12] Consequently, in a city like London, women are 25 per cent more likely than men to 'trip-chain' (combine multiple stops into a bigger journey).[13]

8.6   Crowdsourced nominations for Part W's Alternative List campaign, which aims to increase representation and recognition of women who have made significant contributions to architecture, 2019.

But transport systems are not set up to accommodate this easily, instead prioritising home to workplace journeys, from the periphery to the urban centre. In this way, urban design and infrastructure perpetuates gender inequity.

One solution is to integrate a gender perspective into key decisions, with a specific objective of achieving gender equity. This is called 'gender mainstreaming' and has been included in the UN's strategy for gender equality since 1995. Other global cities are leading the way on this. Vienna has pioneered gender mainstreaming in urban, housing and transport design for 30 years: producing a 'Manual for Gender Mainstreaming in Urban Planning' and pilot projects such as Frauen-Werk-Stadt and Aspern. In Barcelona, Mayor Ada Callou adopted gender mainstreaming in urban design with pedestrianised 'superblocks' and co-designed parks informed by women and girls. We all need to follow their lead: demanding relevant gender disaggregated data and pilot projects.

Underrepresentation in client, funder, procurement and design teams also means we miss out on potentially transformative knowledge and a questioning of the status quo. If we want to treat housing as basic infrastructure and

8.7 Women's Work: London – a map produced by Part W 'that celebrates the contribution of women in shaping the capital'.

8.8   Yẹmí Àládérun, Zoë Berman and Alice Brownfield of Part W, 'a group of women working in architecture, design, infrastructure and construction committed to challenging systems that disadvantage women and calling for gender mainstreaming in the built environment'. www.part-w.com/about.

prioritise equitable design and re-investment in underserved areas, this depends on – or at least acts reciprocally with – equal representation across the built environment sector. We need intersectional diversity across the board; this means rethinking policies on access, recruitment, parental leave, working patterns, equal pay, progression and representation. Many areas of the architecture and construction professions are improving. Those who don't will eventually be left behind.

Another architecture critically rethinks the process of how the built environment comes into being, how it is used, owned, altered, preserved. Who is involved, who is excluded?

This is a call for architects to act *now* – upskilling and using our own agency to respond to wider societal and environmental crises. This means taking conversations about equitable design beyond the confines of the architectural world and ensuring we are working in diverse teams with inclusive processes, and with a focus on the longer-term human and environmental impact of our actions. We must build longer tables, not higher walls.

9

FIELD

BIO-ARTS AS PLATFORM FOR COLLABORATION

Xenia Adjoubei, in collaboration with Supermrin
and Jessica Fertonani Cooke

FIELD AS APPROACH

FIELD is an approach that unites artists, designers, programmers, material researchers and urbanists in exploring grass: its deep history and cultural meanings, its social and economic implications, and its materiality, as texture which can be used to transform institutional spaces, as something to weave, dig out, to plant and dance on. It was founded by the Indian artist, Supermrin, joined by performance artist, Jessica Fertonani Cooke, material designer, Jil Berenblum, and architect and urbanist, Xenia Adjoubei. In this chapter we present FIELD as a practice and as a generator of labour economies which rely on collective artistic production.

The materials we developed through the FIELD project can be used to build, make sculptures and engage communities. They are similar to plastic, but are biodegradable, and have a powerful organic quality, allowing us to juxtapose approaches to urban planning and design with ideas of ecology, identity and land ownership. We have tested the materials in construction through robotic fabrication and explore the role that organic materials and human craft may play in this emergent field.

FIELD is open-source and underpinned by the aims of transforming perceptions and making environmental discourse more inclusive, while elevating voices through artistic and craft production using natural materials. Past projects have involved wide-reaching communities in collective cook-outs and collaborative cooking of biomaterials in domestic kitchens, collective object-making, workshops for all ages, and performative practices and activism to safeguard urban meadows.[1] FIELD promotes environmental awareness through

9.1   Installation view of FIELD, birch [Prove it, day said to night. And night succumbed to the heat of day. There were months where she could not speak on her dark gray light. There were months that the sun shone like blazing fire in the dead of night, nightless nights, we experienced. There were nights when we couldn't dream.], 2022, grass-based bioplastic, two birch trees, 182.88 × 213.36 cm (72 × 84 in).

9.2   FIELD [garden], 2021, turmeric, grass-based biomaterials, 30.48 × 30.48 cm (12 × 12 in).

an experiential critique; it offers an open invitation to imagine new structures and materials for a nature-based ethics.

FIELD AS ATTRIBUTE

Grass is an attribute of any city, present in sports fields, public lawns, park meadows or suburban front lawns that weave together the synthetic landscapes of golf courses and traffic islands. Given its ubiquity, we see grass as an underestimated substrate for new artistic and urban planning interventions.

The lawn is as much a cultural construct as it is a physical surface, and for this reason is deeply political. Lawns are the standard institutionalised carpeting for spaces of leisure and control, from the lawns of city halls and courthouses to colonial sports grounds such as football and cricket pitches, and tennis courts. We blindly accept the presence of lawns because of their almost audacious normalcy.

Grass takes over the body and mind, as Elizabeth Diller and Ricardo Scofidio explored in their 1999 exhibition, *The American Lawn*, at the Canadian Centre for Architecture. In the exhibition, the curators recounted how the 'representational function of the lawn is deciphered: in federal and institutional landscape the lawn is used to symbolise collective solidarity; in corporate culture it is used to represent power and control; in domestic culture it is a battleground between the democratic image of uniformity and the right to self-expression guaranteed by the First Amendment'.[2]

If we were to view grass, not as a 'sinister surface of repressed horror', as Diller and Scofidio describe it, but as a sustainable natural resource abundant in cities, it can become an opportunity for collective creativity and reconstruction, not as a method of control. FIELD proposes grass as an attribute of the city, and a resource to enable citizens to manifest their own ideas of public space, as a connection to nature.

FIELD began in 2020 on the lawn in the Frank H. Ogawa Plaza in front of Oakland City Hall in California where, after extensive conversations with city workers, landscapers, gardeners and mowers, the artist Supermrin received the City Council's approval to create a 'no-mow' lawn for one season. Working with the Oakland Economic and Workforce Development Department, the Public Art Council and the Parks and Recreation Department, Supermrin's aim was to subvert the landscape of 'power and control', and the singularity of the public art which had previously occupied the space, to bring the lawn back to nature, and make its experience an opportunity to pause, listen and reflect in the tall grass. The project also offered a provocation to the city authorities to reflect on their park maintenance policies, which favour industrially produced GM grasses that require constant watering, fertilisation and reseeding, above endemic species of grass.

FIELD AS MATERIAL

Inspired by the idea of the no-mow lawn and the potential of a never-ending and free source of materials, in 2021 FIELD invented a unique grass-based

9.3   A consortium of grass-based biomaterials, created as part of the *Climate Provocations* Pavilions Exhibition, Governors Island, New York, 2021.

9.4   Materials production, from collecting grass clippings to drying, boiling, washing, blending, mixing, cooking and setting.

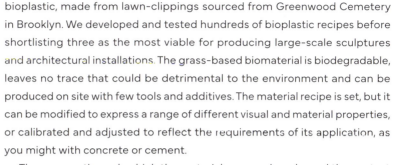

bioplastic, made from lawn-clippings sourced from Greenwood Cemetery in Brooklyn. We developed and tested hundreds of bioplastic recipes before shortlisting three as the most viable for producing large-scale sculptures and architectural installations. The grass-based biomaterial is biodegradable, leaves no trace that could be detrimental to the environment and can be produced on site with few tools and additives. The material recipe is set, but it can be modified to express a range of different visual and material properties, or calibrated and adjusted to reflect the requirements of its application, as you might with concrete or cement.

The process through which the material was produced – and the context in which that work took place – was just as important as the end product. The material was developed in the midst of the COVID-19 pandemic together with industrial designer and material scientist, Jil Berenblum, and with the support of Genspace, a unique Brooklyn-based community biology lab, which makes hands-on life sciences accessible to a wide audience. The pandemic made ideas of decentralisation of supply chains mainstream, so it seemed logical for FIELD to use this moment to develop a set of 'natural plastics', made using readily available kitchen equipment and grass, which as a result could be sourced for free, almost anywhere in the world. This mechanism for the decentralisation of production felt akin to a new era of cottage industry, except that, rather than lace or candlesticks, new materials were being produced in basements and kitchens. We saw this as a powerful call to arms for the possibility – as the New York-based trend analyst, Li Edelkoort, eloquently put it – of a new 'arts-and-crafts century, where manual labour is cherished above everything else'.[3]

FIELD subsequently open-sourced the bioplastic recipes under a Creative Commons license, and we have actively worked to democratise the material science behind the product through workshops that have so far engaged over 300 artists, architects, students and children. We have also organised collective cook-outs for sourcing and making biomaterials, and have made a series of collaborative experimental artworks, which FIELD uses to further test craft techniques. The workshops are not about teaching or learning; rather, they are a method of radicalisation through making, a way to make climate activism accessible to any person of any age or skill level.

In the summer of 2021, FIELD created FIELD [moth] – a 1.2 by 1.5-metre double-curved sculpture, which was modelled in 3D and fabricated using hand extrusion over a Styrofoam mould using two varieties of the grass-based

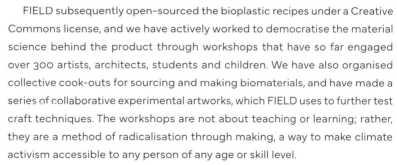

9.5 FIELD [plaza], 2022, turmeric, grass-based biomaterials.

9.6 Installation view of FIELD, birch [Prove it day said to night . . .], 2022, grass-based bioplastic, two birch trees, 182.88 × 213.36 cm (72 × 84 in).

biomaterial. The work was the first large-scale experiment designed to test the biomaterial's weather and time resistance. Despite being made predominantly from grass, the structure has not decayed over the past 18 months, but instead has shrunk and transformed into a material similar to cartilage, which resonates strongly with the idea of bodily flexibility and simultaneous impermanence.

FIELD AS CONCEPT

FIELD can be a map to what is local and global, a natural resource for uncertain urban futures, a generator of bioplastics which, as alternatives to oil-based materials, can support the Fourth Industrial Revolution through open-source robotic fabrication of architectural forms. FIELD can be a building material that offers zero-waste strategies for parks, and improves social cohesion by promoting endemic meadows and collective art production and improving the resilience of cities.

FIELD emphasises the multiple histories of women's work on land, and equally in the home, by turning the kitchen into a laboratory capable of producing an innovative natural plastic or construction material. This unique grass-based biomaterial can be modified to express a range of visual and material properties. It operates as a window into a plant-centric view of the world, where humans can live in and sustain themselves on plants and plant-based products, where architecture is sensitive to its environment and acknowledges a new-found temporality and impermanence in its materiality.

The drawings, sculptures and installations produced by FIELD are fragile, but resilient, visually inviting and richly tactile. These material-inspired works draw attention to the embodied human condition and its inextricable link to nature.

FIELD AS ENVIRONMENT

FIELD is a critique of the urban typology of the manicured civic park, which is replicated in cities across the world, and the billion-dollar industry it advances. Urban grasses are usually homogenous, monocultures of genetically modified seeds that do not flower. They are ecologically unsustainable and require

extensive resources to build and maintain. Comprising over three times the acreage of agricultural corn production, manicured lawns are the single largest irrigated crop in the United States.

Lawn grass has deeply embedded psychological associations with social order and safety: from the traditions of the English Landscape Garden and the gardens of Versailles being a symbol of wealth and political stability, to the American dream of the front lawn reflecting macho one-upmanship and desires for consumer goods. Genetically modified, fertilised and mechanically watered grass occupies over 40 million acres – or two per cent – of the continental United States. The majority of grass is fertilised, which is damaging to the environment and requires excessive watering, which strains an already overstretched water-supply system in an ecosystem prone to extreme weather events, such as droughts, storms and forest fires. Yet in 2023, millions of Americans still hold on to their dream and spend over $30 billion a year on lawn care.

Certain major public institutions and private parks, such as Little Island and Columbia University, have in recent years made concerted efforts to reintroduce endemic species of grass into their landscaping strategies. But the vast majority of public institutions still fail to interrogate unsustainable lawn-seeding as a go-to method of urban landscaping.

Combining large-scale applications and performances which try to rekindle a form of land-memory, FIELD aims to reshape current urban policies by offering

9.7 Grass-based biomaterial structure maquette.

9.8 FIELD [moth], 2021, wood, grass-based biomaterials, 121.92 × 152.4 cm (48 × 60 in).

the 'collective', 'artistic', 'indigenous' and 'ever changing' as new ways of thinking about landscape in public spaces.

FIELD's recent performance, *Braiding FIELD,* in New York City Hall Park in November 2022, interrogated manicured institutional lawns not just on the grounds of ecology, but as representations of a wider problematic of inequity, the rewriting of history and environmental justice. Through such performances, FIELD aims to evoke historic landscapes and allows the urban lawn to become a patchwork map of political issues – contemporary and historic, local and global.

FIELD AS CULTURE

Braiding FIELD is just one of a series of performance pieces that FIELD has realised in public spaces across the world: from a performance on the historic hunting and gathering land of the Lenape on Nut Island (or

Governors Island, as it is now called) in New York City, continuing with *Sleeping, Breast-feeding, Singing, Digging, Mending, Tearing & Weaving*, which was carried out jointly and remotely between Brazil and Wales (with the support of tactileBOSCH), to *Braiding FIELD* itself which was performed by four women of multi-ethnic descent (supported by Franklin Furnace Archive) in New York City Hall Park, which was recently acknowledged to stand on an African slave burial ground.

Across all these works, FIELD has brought people together in order to create new public infrastructures that are sculptural and experiential, utilising the plant we most often walk over to bring to the surface questions around the meaning of land, its deep history and its role as a resting place of imbedded memories. The works are elemental and primordial, much like the biomaterial itself, but they are simple and direct in their message. They allow FIELD to tap into the long tradition of conceptual land-based projects in New York City, such as Mierle Laderman Ukeles's *Touch Sanitation* (1979–80), in which she brought attention to the role that service labour, and female labour, plays in sustaining life,[4] and *Wheatfields for Manhattan* (1982) by Agnes Denes, where, by planting a field of wheat in Battery Park City Landfill, the artist drew attention to inherent paradoxes in capitalist value systems.

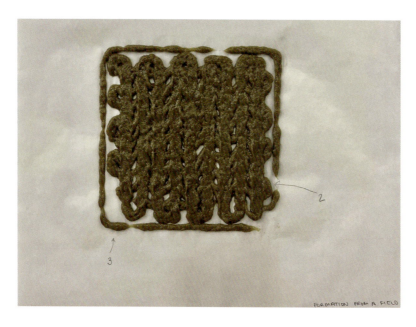

9.9 Complete robotic fabrication using grass-based biomaterial.

9.10 In progress robotic fabrication using grass-based biomaterial.

FIELD AS BUILDING RESOURCE

In 2021, FIELD experimented with using grass as a clean natural resource for construction,[5] and in particular the possibilities of robotic fabrication using extrusion. We developed this method of fabrication in partnership with the Consortium for Research and Robotics, Brooklyn Navy Yard, and it remains unique in showing how scaling using repetitive machine production techniques can yield applications of grass-based plastic on an architectural scale, at the very least in facade systems and insulation.

Over history, the discovery of new materials has yielded new architectural languages and new ways of generating form. FIELD argues that the exterior and interior application of materials should not be dictated by the design of the building, but the other way around: by the capabilities of the material itself. This can be seen in the growing number of applications of mycelium to architecture, or in the knitted architecture of Sean Ahlquist or Zaha Hadid Architects – and stands in contrast to the highly aestheticised work of Neri Oxman, for example, which focuses on aesthetic experience as a way of bringing new worlds into focus.

FIELD's invention of a new material and trans-disciplinary practices, which glide between the scientific and the artistic, the real and the imagined, generates important new aesthetic and production challenges for architecture. It poses the questions: 'So what if it doesn't look slick and shiny and finished, and capable of resisting the elements? So what, if it doesn't make you feel comfortable and protected and warm, like traditional building materials?' FIELD sits within the discourse of closed loop systems and EcoRedux architecture, developed by Lydia Kallipoliti,[6] which are not always beautiful, but take scarcity of resources as a given and a central driver to the development of new spatial languages.

9.11   FIELD performance, 2022, grass-based biomaterial, tree branches, 182.88 × 304.8 cm (72 × 120 in).

FIELD AS SYMBOL

The combination of research, praxis and critical proposition set out by FIELD poses a strong argument that artistic production can situate humanity in a 'New Cosmology', as set out by Bruno Latour.[7] FIELD's approach reveals the connection between our material experiences of nature and burgeoning technologies, such as robotics and material science, in order to draw a new kind of relational diagram between the two, bringing contemporary technological discourses into relationship with the planet's most ancient memories and new forms of ecological planetary thinking.

FIELD allows us to locate architectural and artistic production within an increasingly politicised context, and to do so in a constructive way. FIELD is a symbol manifest, a solidified metaphor, which opens the opportunity to experience deep histories and collective memories.

Each member of the FIELD collective brings a different cultural background to the project, from India to Brazil, the United States to Europe. But what unites its members is an ongoing practice that places identity and belonging at its heart. These are some of the most precious yet volatile concepts of our time and, by building up multi-faceted knowledges and experiences about them, FIELD becomes an important and powerful tool for designers or policy-makers for a world in flux.

RESETS

10

ARCHITECTURE

ABOLISHED OR ABOLITIONIST?

V. Mitch McEwen

From where we are in this century, it is clear that architecture is part of the problem.

In the United States, construction materials, including stone, gravel and sand, account for around three-quarters of raw materials use.[1] In addition to this direct extraction, materials classified as industrial mineral commodities get deployed in building materials consumed by construction – cement for ready-mix concrete, gypsum in drywall and plaster, and soda ash in the production of glass.[2] Hundreds of millions of tons of industrial minerals create buildings that then require multiple times their weight in gravel and sand to nestle them into extended road networks. These new roads and highways connect the new construction to jobs, schools, hospitals, airports – the old construction that is recursively insufficient and requires this supplement of constant sprawl. The statistics in the Center for Sustainable Systems' factsheet are aggregated and reported nationally, but the spatial pattern reproduces itself without regard to national borders.[3]

So many buildings built today are isolated, ugly, flimsy, segregating and frequently undesired by local communities. They require heating and cooling through systems that burn coal and other fossil fuels. They further entrench a polluting and exclusive car-centric culture. They flood and are easily damaged in hurricanes, with such extreme weather events more common because of climate change. Meanwhile too many of us remain unhoused, evicted, precarious. Millions of tons of raw materials are extracted from the ground to build a world that doesn't work for us.

At the same time, the carbon emitted by the buildings themselves continues to increase.[4] In 2020, 70 per cent of new homes built in the United States were single-family houses.[5] The pattern trumps distinctions between luxury and

10.1 'I didn't want to design an object. I wanted to … tell a story, really, of Black fugitivity and Black liberation…. What R:R is positing, is that with the knowledge that we already have we could be building in a way that we don't know yet.' Detail of the 3D-printed architectural forms of R:R, 2021. www.moma.org/audio/playlist/312/4049.

poverty, suburb and exurb. The pattern of sprawl and single-family houses is also repeated in Sub-Saharan Africa and in the largest cities in Latin America.[6] Urban planners call this the 'metropolitan centre–periphery pattern', in which 'the periphery has been shifted to outer peripheral rings'.[7] Building construction today means bigger and ever more materially inefficient buildings farther and farther away from each other. How is this happening? Is this a pattern, an algorithm, a system? How can it be undone?

10.2   Mycelium composites created by the Black Box Research Group at Princeton University School of Architecture, 2021.

SAYING NO TO ARCHITECTURE

A century ago, in the year 1923, a certain Swiss-French architect who had recently renamed himself Le Corbusier published a manifesto that unfurled many of the patterns and tendencies that continue to define the built world as we know it today. *Vers une architecture* – published in English as *Towards a New Architecture*, though literally translating as 'Towards an Architecture' – heralded, among other examples, American engineering and its civil engineering outputs – grain silos in Buffalo especially – as the future of architectural form and methods.

In the final chapter, Le Corbusier offered a choice of two directions for society and for the world: '*C'est une question de bâtiment qui est à la clé de*

10.3 Mycelium composites in the Black Box Research Group's biofabrication shed. The repurposed typical wood shed is insulated with hempcrete, 2021.

l'équilibre rompu aujourd'hui: architecture ou révolution.[8] [It is the question of building which lies at the root of the social unrest today: architecture or revolution.]

In the binary terms of Le Corbusier's question, the recently independent socialist nations and the racially segregated nations in the Americas came together in the 20th century in choosing architecture, rather than revolution. Le Corbusier's manifesto of modernism fundamentally changed our approach to making and remaking cities, with vast swathes of many cities demolished and stitched back together with parking lots and highways. In simple terms, concrete proliferated.

Let us take stock of what this choice resulted in. We arrive, a hundred years later, in a situation where, according to the United Nations' IPCC Report, buildings accounted for over 30 per cent of CO_2 emissions in 2019.[9] Urban planners now admit that modernist-inspired urban renewal programmes around the world were largely a disaster, displacing people of colour, dismantling networks of public transit, and destroying walkable neighbourhoods, downtowns and tree-lined sidewalks for the benefits of automotive parking.

Posing Le Corbusier's question again a hundred years later, it may be time to choose differently.

WHAT WOULD IT MEAN TO ABOLISH ARCHITECTURE?

A critique, a map of resistance, needs to be made. What does abolition abolish? This, of course, is an ongoing question.

>
> abolish award-winning masterplans
> abolish zoning police power
> abolish form-based code
> abolish their lovely new building
> abolish architectural character
> abolish drywall
> abolish luxury enclaves
> abolish cul-de-sacs
> abolish the wildland–urban Interface
> abolish speculative real estate
> abolish sub-contracting
> abolish the in/formal binary
> abolish architectural licensing
> abolish the starchitect
> abolish the carceral logic of displacement, eviction, and erasure

There are many conflicting allegiances within architecture, so that architectural energy could be readily marshalled towards abolishing various of the items in the list (or grouping them together into paradigms – architectural character on one side, drywall on the other, and so on). But looking at the list collectively, a bigger question emerges: does architecture itself need to be abolished to participate in the abolitionist framework? After all, architecture is the common thread from the auction block through recursive urban renewal.

The paradox of the architecture or revolution dichotomy is that it doubly erases revolution. Knowing the 20th-century history of Le Corbusier's high-rise ideas being translated into public housing for the poor and middle class, in hindsight, the dichotomy is often interpreted as a reckoning with the masses of previously colonised and dispossessed people. The notion being that if the dispossessed were not provided with architecture – in the form of high-density urban apartment buildings surrounded by some form of urban landscape – they would revolt.

10.4 Image from the author's work, 'R:R, Republica: Reconstructed', which was displayed in the exhibition *Reconstructions: Architecture and Blackness in America*, 27 February – 31 May 2021, at the Museum of Modern Art, New York.

Either way, rhetorically in the text, or historically in the built work, the choice of architecture or revolution was implicitly presented, then, to the coloniser or the dispossessing state. Choose architecture, to mitigate against revolution. Contain the people before they resist. And the result? A built environment completely unprepared and unwilling to adapt to climate change, and worse, deeply implicated in the extractive economies and colonised systems that have brought about the climate crisis.

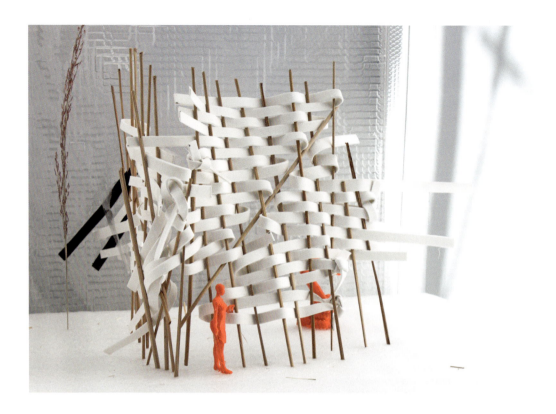

If Le Corbusier railed against the late 19th-century Beaux-Arts training and its irrelevance for the machine era of work and living for being limited to decoration, obsessed with styles, too slow to adapt to the innovative techniques available in material and construction in the early 20th century, then a similar critique can be levied at architecture again today. Today the construction industry is the only large industry that is less productive in this century than it was in 1960.[10] This means that with the same labour force, time and tools, a house built today will actually be lower quality than one built in 1960, irrespective of land prices or location, and despite advances in materials, instruments, technology and skills.

The odd thing is that, even without the statistics, we know this already. Just from experience, we know that relative quality in an entire industry has declined, while almost every other industry has gained efficacy from scientific knowledge (medicine and pharmaceuticals) or mechanised production (electronics) or digital production and information flow (mapping, messaging, dating, media).

Today, the profession and discipline of architecture – not only its practices but its educational mores and institutions, its civic and cultural dimensions

10.5 'Republica is … an idea that is authored by an artist named Kristina Kay Robinson, who is a native of New Orleans and my idea partner. It's a place that emerges from a key event, which is the largest rebellion against slavery in North America [in 1811] … Republica is, effectively, New Orleans in an alternate reality, where the rebellion is successful.' www. moma.org/audio/ playlist/312/4049.

– are woefully out of step with the social and material changes that people and planet are undergoing. The difference this time is that architecture finds itself overly entangled with the industrialisation that Le Corbusier promoted as a solution. The relentless thirst for the new and innovative, along with the obsessions over surface and mass, are irrelevant and incompatible with the shift to a degrowth economic system, a just transition to non-extractive economies and a radical move away from fossil fuels and automobiles.

What would replace architecture, then, after its five centuries or so of authority in the built environment? What modes of spatial practice emerge when we consider the plethora of overlaps between decentralised technologies and democratic protest? What modes of spatial production are already happening in activism or collective acts of resistance and fugitivity? What Black knowledges might make architecture as we know it obsolete?

Rather than turning towards another architecture, an abolitionist mode would have to consider what modes of building and unbuilding, thinking and collaborating, would participate in making an abolitionist world, another world, more probable. Another world has to be prioritised before another architecture. At the same time, those of us who believe ourselves to be architects have a responsibility to situate ourselves in relation to another world through our specific knowledges, whether spatial, material, social or technological. This means critiquing architectural entanglements and separations, and, just as importantly, creating and nurturing alternatives to architecture.

BUILDING WITH YOU

Building with, in Black parlance, presents an an-architectural paradigm for making space.

To draw *building with* onto the space of this page requires shifting to more embodied use of language. *Building with* inflects process onto and through relations. *Building with* may be understood ontologically, but not objectively. As Katherine McKittrick writes: 'Geographic alternatives are best displayed through communicative acts – geographic expressions that . . . cite/site underacknowledged black geographies.'[11] The ontology invoked by *building with* would be narrative-oriented, not object-oriented.

The geographic alternative of *building with* can be sited in music. A citation from American singer and songwriter Anthony Hamilton makes this evident. It is no accident this arrives succinctly in the form of a love song – *Since I Seen't You* – since *building with* also invokes love.[12] Hamilton's brilliance is in a kind of Black immersion, the condensed beauty of an everyday Black experience, the exceptional beauty of an everyday Black love. (Another song on the same album is titled *Cornbread, Fish & Collard Greens*.)

You're 'bout the flyest thang

Fly, in Black parlance, means visually appealing, but Hamilton shifts this to both flight and transparency. 'This love is see through', writes Hamilton, also like air. Is air transparent, or is air what we *see through* – bringing sight closer to movement, as in I can see through the act of breathing? Imagine the air you are breathing in right now being part of what enables you to sit with this text and think with it. There's an environment staged that makes the love in Hamilton's song seeable and breathable. One can think of the mantra *Black is beautiful* and how saying this out loud in a white supremacist society could be necessary to make Black self-love and Black desire possible to oneself. A political mantra, images conceived in Black politics, may make Black love transparent to oneself, as desire or self-love.

We been peoples … you're my equal … Your conversation is liberating

Liberation and equality are paired with the becoming of peoples.[13] This see-through love circulates in a fresh air environment that also sustains democracy, at least between the singer and this loved one, if nowhere else. Wanting to *build with* implies this breathing democratic people-becoming in love.

In Hamilton's voice, the refrains 'And I want, wanna build with you' and 'I want to be with you' sound similar. 'Your conversation is liberating.' The conversation generates a liberatory potential, a form of politics. In Hamilton's ode to the *building with* of a Black love, this relating also entwines with becoming *peoples* and being *equals*. A democracy is presented here, through communicative action. Where European neo-Enlightenment philosophers such as Jürgen Habermas fundamentally presume communication becomes political action through rationality, Hamilton presents love as the (see-through) medium of communicative action.

10.6 The architecture volumes of 'R:R, Republica: Reconstructed' are rendered as 3D-printed space frames, and the soft ground is modelled with a mix of canvas, acetate, cosmetic glitter and wood shavings.

WHAT WOULD IT MEAN TO ABOLISH ARCHITECTURE AND *BUILD WITH*?

That is the question that animates my work (figs 10.1 and 10.3–10.7) and the work I support in this abolitionist movement. It would imply being able to *draw* from our feelings of being racially profiled by the police, for example, of being stopped and frisked, of being hungry or abandoned – as much or more than our feelings of comfort and intellectual exuberance in the studio. This would not be a matter of translating feeling into design. This would entail radically re-orienting how we choose to do work, whom we work for, how we both imagine and prioritise what we do. It also eliminates and explodes that presumed we and demands the constitution of another becoming peoples (in and through the collective production of buildings, shared space and infrastructure).

Over and over again, it is impossible to continue to see architecture as an innocent bystander. In the midst of movements to abolish the police, there can be heard a demand that any practical knowledge investigate not only its direct relationship to incarceration and jails (architects are still designing jails[14]), but also the systemic relationship to the plantation. The plantation – as abolitionists teach us[15] – is the birthplace of the carceral state.

10.7 'The bamboo [is] a material that is very strong ... The bamboo with the felt woven around it is a building method that could replace carpentry, building upon the skills of someone who would braid hair, the skills of someone who would produce textiles, someone who's familiar with patterns.' www. moma.org/audio/ playlist/312/4049.

Architecture cannot change how anything is built without materials and labour participating. Architecture cannot change how anything is thought without social formations, language and cultures also changing. To ask how we arrive at this material built reality and how we might change it, then, demands more than a sense of architecture, an understanding of racial capitalism. An abolitionist architecture or an abolition of architecture demands a spatial understanding of racial capitalism through Black study.

Where architecture understands logistics as an aspect of rationalisation, Black study traces logistics to the slave ship. Where architecture sees a series of movements that significantly change how buildings are designed – from the Beaux-Arts to modernism to postmodernism to deconstructivism – Black study sees spatial logics of profiteering and erasure that remain remarkably consistent from the plantation to today. The question is not 'architecture or revolution', but whether architecture itself can be 'abolished or abolitionist'.

11

HOME REVOLUTION

EQUALITY BEYOND REPRESENTATION
IN THE WORK OF EDIT

Marianna Janowicz

The phrase 'towards another architecture' raises two immediate questions: what that 'another architecture' might be and also how we find a way 'towards' it. Destinations are only meaningful when we have a clear sense of the routes and methods that can take us there, which also means knowing where we are starting from. For architecture, the starting points are the demographics, practices and underlying assumptions that characterise the profession today, but also, and more specifically, the particular sites where change is most likely to take root. Audre Lorde's famous 'master's tools' will not help us dismantle, or not even reform, the master's house.

All too often, the architectural industry feels too slow to change; equality and diversity of the profession are stuck in the past, and working practices appear almost comically antiquated compared to more progressive fields, creative and otherwise. The famous quote, commonly misattributed to Einstein, says: 'Insanity is repeating the same mistake over and over again and expecting different results.'[1] And yet, in architecture in particular, we seem to insist on employing the same methods while aiming for different, new results.

Even a cursory look at the data reveals that architectural practice today – as understood in the traditional sense and regulated by institutions such as the ARB (Architects Registration Board) and RIBA – is still dominated by men. The ARB's statistics for 2019 reveal that 71 per cent of those on the register were male and 29 per cent were female. When compared to industries such as law or medicine, which also require multiple degrees and professional validation, architecture lags behind. But the issue, and its resolution, is far from simple. It isn't simply about bringing the stats to 50/50, creating more 'girl bosses' in a patriarchal world. It is about transforming the system from the ground up.

11.1 What architectural opportunities lie in shared resources and reproductive labour? Kinfrastructure, collage, 2021.

If we want different results – better buildings, decarbonisation, equality – why do we insist on practising the same way? With awards that most commonly champion western, lone genius figures, a profession riven by hierarchical structures, and systems of monitoring membership which overlook fundamental intersectional differences, architecture as currently constituted simply perpetuates the existing way of doing things.[2]

Setting up Edit as a group of women was always about moving beyond representation. The assumption tends to be that Edit is a feminist collective just because it is formed solely of women members, but whilst we all consider ourselves feminists and enjoy the sisterhood, the 'feminism' in our name refers to the methods we aspire to employ. Inspired by practices such as the feminist design co-operative Matrix, or more recently Assemble, Resolve and muf architecture/art, Edit takes on a name that does not identify any individuals and sets out to build a collective and non-hierarchical mode of practice. In pragmatic terms, this means unlearning some tropes absorbed in architecture school, spending long hours in conversations and endeavouring to distribute money fairly, valuing the less glamorous administration work on a par with design.

Whilst feminism is Edit's starting point, positioning in the world and the primary mode of enquiry, it is only one of the methods that can enable 'another architecture'. In recent years, the appearance of alternative practices and activist groups has been testament to the growing discontentment with the status quo. In Britain alone, groups such as Black Females in Architecture, FAME Collective, Part W and Asian Architects Association have created their own platforms as alternatives to the often homogenous and uninspiring professional bodies. Future Architects Front leads the way on workers' rights through its campaigning, writing and excellent use of social media. Projects such as Afterparti, POoR Collective, DisOrdinary Architecture, Dis Collective or New Architecture Writers highlight the breadth of human experiences that have been largely overlooked in architectural production – whether it's class, sexuality, race or disability. Further afield, the Catalan co-operative Lacol and its experimental housing project La Borda creates a tangible connection between the mode of practice and the possibility of another architecture.

At Edit, the critique of architecture begins, in a feminist fashion, at home. The family home remains a strong and established trope today, its organisation often taken for granted or perceived as neutral. Author and academic Helen Hester uses the term 'Domestic Realism' to describe 'the phenomenon whereby the isolated dwelling (and the concomitant privatisation of household labour)

11.2   *Gross Domestic Product*, a vacuum cleaner which must be operated by three people working simultaneously, was developed for the 2019 Oslo Architecture Triennale.

11.3   *Gross Domestic Product* (2019) is designed to question the assumption that domestic work is best done individually.

becomes so accepted and commonplace that it is almost impossible to imagine life being organised through any other form'.[3] Much of Edit's work has set out to reject Domestic Realism and begin imagining other ways of organising social reproduction. If feminist methods are about tracing structures of power, then that is what we attempt to do, starting in the nuclear family home and following its sphere of influence which ripples out far beyond it.

Today, the standardised model of housing for the 'family' (usually meaning a heterosexual, nuclear family) is being reproduced and marketed as the most natural, default type of dwelling, but contemporary social structures no longer comply with that typical model. People living alone and in house shares are two growing trends in the UK. Edit's *Gross Domestic Product*, a vacuum cleaner which must be operated by three people simultaneously, was conceived in opposition to the privatisation and individualisation of reproductive labour, but also to question the hegemony and wastefulness of private property manifested in the popular ownership of home electrical devices (figs 11.2 and 11.3). Similarly to Daniel Barber, who imagines a world after comfort as a world in which we must abandon the luxuries of individually controlled thermal conditions,[4] Edit imagines a future in which we pry ourselves away from the comforts of single-family living and consumption. We propose a move towards unfamiliar waters of alternative kinship structures and the discomforts of sharing. We envision life in capitalist ruins but not as a dystopian vision – *Gross Domestic Product* may be a speculative provocation but it embodies some of the joy and optimism with which we propose to tackle these challenges. To echo Barber's words,

11.4   Across the Global North, drying laundry outside is legally regulated and socially policed in a bid to preserve the appearance of the built environment. *Laundry Day* film still, 2021.

11.5   *Laundry Day* (2021) is a short film directed, shot and produced by Edit for MAXXI in Rome.

'discomfort is an opportunity'. After crisis comes reinvention and rebuilding. But it cannot happen by tokenistically showcasing and selectively incorporating marginalised voices. Rather, it will require ceding of power and a home revolution, which will potentially involve some growing pains.

Naturally, there is a link between methods and outcomes, and a conservative profession is bound to reproduce obsolete models and preserve established power dynamics. There is hope in the productive frictions arising from groups opposing and questioning the professional bodies, working conditions and processes within architecture. There is hope that, inspired by these new movements, we will be able to imagine working and living otherwise. In order to imagine, we start by telling ourselves different stories. As Gloria Anzaldúa wrote: 'Nothing happens in the "real" world unless it first happens in the images in our heads.'[5] I propose that to establish another architecture, it is useful to start at home – whether it is the patriarchal, private family house or the home of the profession. Both uphold power dynamics which have wide-reaching influence. Would putting our house(s) in order help open up more channels for change?

In *Laundry Day*, a short film made by Edit in the summer of 2021, we carried wet laundry across central London and hung it on a washing line above the entrance to the RIBA building in 66 Portland Place (figs 11.4 and 11.5). The resulting images bring together the converging and conflicting notions of home and institution, privacy and publicity (see fig.11.1). A three-person vacuuming

11.6 The exhibition, *How We Live Now: Reimagining Spaces with Matrix Feminist Design Co-operative*, was designed around a table – a space to gather, linger, organise, read.

"Buildings do not control our lives. They reflect the dominant values in our society... ideas about women, about our 'proper place', about what is private and what is public activity, about which things should be kept separate and which to put together."
Matrix

11.7 Curated by Jon Astbury and Jos Boys, and designed by Edit, *How We Live Now: Reimagining Spaces with Matrix Feminist Design Co-operative* was an exhibition exploring the work of Matrix, held at the Barbican Centre in London (17 May 2021 – 30 January 2022).

party and a group laundry performance may appear like a strange proposition for another architecture, but at least they are not the futility of trying the same thing over and over again. Only by beating our own path will we find a route leading 'towards another architecture'.

11.8   *How We Live Now: Making Spaces in the North East with Matrix Feminist Design Co-operative* was presented in Newcastle, UK by the Farrell Centre and Newcastle University's School of Architecture, Planning and Landscape, in association with Newcastle Contemporary Art and the Barbican Centre (6 May – 23 July 2022).

11.9   Designed by Edit using the modular timber system first developed for the Barbican, the exhibition featured films, drawings, photos, and architectural models, as well as posters, practice documents and press clippings, that documented Matrix's approaches to design that aimed to empower groups often excluded in the design of buildings.

12

TOWARDS A QUEER ARCHITECTURAL HISTORY

Joshua Mardell

Architectural history has a long history of exclusion – of subjects, spaces and constituencies of people deemed unworthy of its attention. Queer by sensibility, I am interested in helping to redress historiographical injustices of this kind – as informed by my own marginalised status as queer and working class – both in the focus of my work and in the very act of pursuing a career in architectural history in which queer themes have remained sidelined, and where an inequitable social structure and elitist culture is still endemic.[1]

One of the subjects of my research has been the 'barefoot' architect Pat Crooke (1927–2018), who has hitherto stood outside the dominant narratives of modernism, thanks to his adopting an approach to practice that could not fit within them. On leaving the Architectural Association in 1952, Crooke spent his career assisting with self-build housing in Peru and Colombia, developing an alternative approach to architecture in which he sought, as Norman Potter put it, 'to ally oneself with a do-it-yourself anti-professional working stance – architecture without architects'.[2] Crooke's 'Modulor Monkey', illustrated in the editorial of the student magazine *PLAN* in 1950, speaks for his anarchism of turning architecture on its head (fig.12.2).

The eccentric and off-beam Buckler dynasty of 19th-century Gothic Revival architects are another subject of my research and offer a further case in point. Such *non*-salient, and self-consciously *non*-innovatory, figures, have been all but ignored in histories of the period, yet have a story that is vital to tell. Aloof in their own time, the Bucklers served themselves a historiographical death sentence in the 20th century when narratives of 'progress' prevailed. Figure 12.1 shows the third-generation scion Charles Alban Buckler (1824–1905), Catholic architect and Knight of Malta, bedizened in full heraldic regalia on his visiting card, appearing almost sacerdotal – a camp icon. It is quite as though

12.1   Portrait of Charles Alban Buckler as Surrey Herald Extraordinary in tabard and Collar of Esses, c.1880, photographer unknown.

12.2   Pat Crooke's 'Modulor Monkey', illustrated on the editorial page of *PLAN*, no.7, the journal of the Architectural Students' Association, 1950.

the Bucklers' obsession with the past was a kind of sickness, an intellectual form of Romanov haemophilia. Totally estranged from the rest of the profession (especially his contemporary George Edmund Street), Buckler created his own temporality and his own realm of desire in a world of oppression.

I am also interested in recovering stories from buildings that cannot hope to merit listing or inclusion in survey literature or the mainstream architectural press. By this I mean the seemingly 'second rate' (as progressive narratives might hold), the common or garden, the ephemeral and transient, the appropriated and the undesigned. They hold extraordinary potential for unfolding more holistic truths, and offer autonomy from controlled discourses and institutional structures of architectural critique.

This outlook fed into *Queer Spaces: An Atlas of LGBTQIA+ Places and Stories* (RIBA Publishing, 2022), a book I co-edited with Adam Nathaniel

Furman, which stands as a provocative challenge to the subjects worthy of architectural history's scrutiny, the constituencies it speaks to, and the practitioners who speak for it. It seeks to create a sense of belonging and continuity for queer themes within the architectural world, hitherto lacking an accessible lineage. Sensitive to a wide range of identities, experiences and cultural traditions, the 'atlas' resists accepted epistemes of mapping, such as the prevailing architectural tradition – in the Venturi-Scott Brown mode – of approaching phenomena as a tourist and taking authorial ownership over it. Rather, each author has their own definitions, experiences, ideas and stories, thereby opening up possibilities and broadening inclusion in the representation of queer spaces, rather than narrowing it.

The elitist and socially exclusive make-up of architectural history might well explain why certain themes and subjects have failed to enter scholarly awareness. It might well also be why, in spite of extraordinary equality, diversity and inclusion initiatives which aim to redress the situation, questions of socio-economic disadvantages are still routinely ignored. Who, anyway, are the *working-class* architectural historians, and why is it so controversial to come out as one? The residues of British architectural history as a service industry for an elite – memorably caricatured by Reyner Banham as the 'I-dined-with-the-Earl' school of architectural history – still hold sway.[3] Banham was in many ways the exception who proved the rule, compelled, as he later was in his subsequent defence of attacks from snobby Italian architects, 'to clarify [...] my credentials, as some [...] seem to be questioning my right to speak. I come from a working-class background'.[4]

Today, the questions remain of how much architectural history still is, or projects itself as being, an exclusive club, such as the self-perpetuating imagery of the Young Georgians – white, wealthy and, by implication, ostracising (fig.12.3)? And how, instead, might architectural history become a force for good, inclusive of, and relevant to, diverse constituencies? A significant barrier to answering the latter question is the fact that those from lower socio-economic backgrounds remain simply less likely to participate in the practice of architectural history. As Samuel Medina has put it of the American architectural context, those who survive in the first place 'are often overworked, underpaid, and forced to adapt to the peripatetic, pauperised conditions of adjunct life'.[5] Without a plurality of experiences and perspectives, how can we expect anything like an equivalent richness in architectural histories? If we are serious about finding a way towards 'another' architecture, then it is vital that we have a truly inclusive understanding

12.3 Johan Zoffany, *Three Sons of John, 3rd Earl of Bute*, c.1763–4, oil on canvas, 100.9 × 126 cm (39 ¾ × 48 ⅝ in). Used as publicity material for the Young Georgians at the Georgian Group.

of its past, one that instrumentalises a queer approach to effect the radical restructuring of architectural history as a discipline, decentring its canons and undoing its perpetuating hierarchies. Another architecture requires another architectural history.

UNTOWARD ARCHITECTURE

Adam Nathaniel Furman

Moving 'towards' implies monodirectional progress, a forceful vector pushing everyone and everything inevitably towards one singular positive goal, towards one, better place. But who is that place for, who decides what form it takes, and what of those for whom it would not be better but worse?

The queer experience of architecture has never been an ism, or a movement 'moving towards' a utopia of architect-defined communal harmony. If anything, it is a negation of the supposed progressive directionality of modernism, the idea that there is a single, unitary answer to all of society's problems that can be encompassed and achieved with communal unanimity.

Queerness itself is a rebuke to that drive for order, the totalitarian-dressed-as-helpful impulse to fix and codify and pin-down, the paternal attitude of

12.4   Adam Nathaniel Furman, axonometric of the imaginary queer city of Capreesh, 2022.

12.5   Adam Nathaniel Furman, *View of the Liberal Archive*, a proposal for a new kind of civic building for London, 2020.

12.6   Adam Nathaniel Furman, *View of the Liberal Archive*, a proposal
for a new kind of civic building for London, 2020.

benevolent control that powers architectural thinking. There is nothing more dangerous than those who believe they have the answers for everyone else, and who are driven by a sense of charitable righteousness on behalf of those 'others'.

We are not passively waiting for architects to save us from ourselves and from the world with their Existenzminimums, their Streets-in-the-Skies, Community Co-designs, Carbon Negatives or their Passivhauses.

Queerness in architecture has always existed on the margins, evolving precariously in the gaps between heavily policed spaces of decorum and shared direction in which everyone must conform to social and professional norms. Like strange flora, it flourishes under a different kind of light, in lacunae, away from the normative gaze.

Queers and our lifestyles, our sexuality, our aesthetics and often our very existence have been antithetical to an architectural environment that sets specific priorities at each given historic moment, and dismisses everything that isn't seen as contributing towards the resolution of that issue as being superfluous, superficial, a distraction, egregious.

The obsessive and paranoid drive to enforce decorum on others, to move towards a sanitised, 'healthy' society, was best exemplified by the Labouchere Amendment (Section 11 of the Criminal Law Amendment Act 1885), which defined British relations to queer deviance for 70 years:

> *Any male person who, in public or private, commits, or is a party to the commission of, or procures, or attempts to procure the commission by any male person of, any act of gross indecency with another male person, shall be guilty of a misdemeanour, and being convicted thereof, shall be liable at the discretion of the Court to be imprisoned for any term not exceeding two years, with or without hard labour.*[6]

The stipulation 'in public or private' was key: in one act of legislation the government removed the right to privacy for a specific minority, catastrophically reducing the space available away from the normative – and now terrorising – hetero gaze.

The fear of deviance, of 'unproductive', gender-ambiguous queers without families and progeny, manifests itself in a new and powerful obsession with the aesthetics of homosexuality. Interiors – for the first time suddenly open to public scrutiny for signs of illegal homosocial activity – became the primary means of social speculation on the acceptability or otherwise of its occupants.

12.7 Adam Nathaniel Furman, *Proud Little Pyramid*, an installation in Granary Square, King's Cross, London, 2021.

Too many objects, too much pattern, too much enjoyment in the material delights of the interior could lead to social ostracisation at best, and prison at worst. Queerness and its visual and spatial expression, even in private – in fact, *especially* in private – became the primary symbol of everything perceived as wrong with a supposedly degenerate era.

Modernism's foundational horror of queer and feminine sensuality and aesthetics built its edifice of hectoring moralisation directly on the principles of the totalitarian, cleansing gaze first applied by the Labouchere Amendment.

No strange light, no bizarre flora. No space for anything that is non-productive, non-problem-solving, non-beneficial in the manner defined by the status quo of a vicious heterodoxy.

Nothing that is not towards *their* goals – their goals that always and inevitably erase *us*.

Queerness does not solve problems; it doesn't move towards anything. Queerness – in architecture and otherwise – is a refusal to accept an existence trapped within the value judgments of a narcissistic and sociopathic minority who demand that their goals be everyone else's goals. It is looking back at the past to reconstruct histories that were built on the desire to control and exclude. It is looking sideways across the world to create families and kinships that build a chorus of voices disassembling the edifices of oppression.

Queer architecture is entirely and incandescently *UNTOWARD*.

NOTES

INTRODUCTION:
ARCHITECTURE *AND* REVOLUTION

1   Le Corbusier, *Towards a New Architecture*, trans. Frederick Etchells (1931), Dover Publications, Inc., New York, 1986, p.3.

2   ibid., p.8.

3   ibid., p.289.

4   This introduction draws from several previously published articles: 'Multiform and the Legacies of Post-Modernism', *Jencks Foundation*, February 2022, www.jencksfoundation.org/explore/text/what-is-was-post-modern-multiform-and-the-legacies-of-post-modernism; 'Multiform is the architectural manifestation of our present moment', *Dezeen*, 25 February 2021, www.dezeen.com/2021/02/25/multiform-architecture-style-owen-hopkins-opinion/; and 'The Forensic Effect', *Icon*, no.187, January 2019, pp 22–24.

5   Marie-Louise Richards, 'Pedagogies of power: education within and without the institution', *The Architectural Review*, 1 September 2022, www.architectural-review.com/essays/keynote/pedagogies-of-power-education-within-and-without-the-institution.

6   Lorenzo Marsili, 'What will life after globalisation look like? The Venice Biennale may hold the answer', 18 June 2023, www.theguardian.com/commentisfree/2023/jun/18/venice-biennale-globalisation-china-cultural-colonialism.

7   Charles Jencks, 'Death for Rebirth', in *Post-Modernism on Trial*, Architectural Design, London, 1990, p.9.

8   Lesley Lokko, 'Agents of Change', Introduction to *Biennale Architettura 2023: The Laboratory of the Future* (The 18th International Architecture Exhibition), 2023, www.labiennale.org/en/architecture/2023/introduction-lesley-lokko.

9   'Technology and human rights: an uneasy relationship?', *Goldsmiths Law Blog*, 16 December 2018, https://sites.gold.ac.uk/law/technology-and-human-rights-an-uneasy-relationship/.

1   LEARNING FROM THE VERNACULAR IN SENEGAL: THE ARCHITECTURE OF WOROFILA

1   '93 % DES CONSTRUCTIONS À DAKAR SE FONT SANS ARCHITECTE', *Seneplus*, 14 February 2019, https://www.seneplus.com/developpement/93-des-constructions-dakar-se-font-sans-architecte.

2   Article 6 of the Law 21-22 relative to Architecture and the Exercise of the Profession, Senegalese Government, 2 March 2021.

3   World Green Building Council, September 2019, Report, *Bringing embodied carbon upfront: coordinated action for the building and construction sector to tackle embodied carbon*, https://worldgbc.s3.eu-west-2.amazonaws.com/wp-content/uploads/2022/09/22123951/WorldGBC_Bringing_Embodied_Carbon_Upfront.pdf.

4   Pierre Friedlingstein, et al., 'Global Carbon Budget 2021', *Earth Systems Science Data*, vol.14, no.4, 1917–2005, 2022, https://doi.org/10.5194/essd-14-1917-2022.

5   Article 6 of the Law 21-22 relative to Architecture and the Exercise of the Profession, Senegalese Government, 2 March 2021.

6   The principle of Asymmetrical Parallelism is also visible in Senghor's Dakar home, later Musée Senghor. Built in 1978 and designed by French architect Fernand Bonamy, the building is inspired by Sudano-Sahelian buildings, but also by Steven Spielberg's 1975 movie, *Jaws*. See Gaëlle Picot,

'Musée Senghor à Dakar, à la rencontre de l'homme de culture', *Le Petit Journal*, 15 November 2018, https://lepetitjournal.com/dakar/a-voir-a-faire/musee-senghor-dakar-la-rencontre-de-lhomme-de-culture-244339.

3   FROM CAUTIONARY TALES TO STORIES OF ACTIVE HOPE: THE MORE-THAN-HUMAN WORK OF SUPERFLUX

1   These projects received funding from the European Union's Horizon 2020 research and innovation programme under grant agreement No 870759.

5   TOWARDS A LIQUID ARCHITECTURE

1   New Zoo, *Introduction to the Metaverse: New Zoo Trend Report*, 2021, https://resources.newzoo.com/hubfs/Reports/Free_Metaverse_Report_Newzoo.pdf.
2   Shumon Basar, Winy Maas and Philip Rosedale, The John Edwards Lecture, Tate Modern, London, November 2010. Organised by the Architecture Foundation, https://vimeo.com/19083999.

8   BUILD LONGER TABLES, NOT HIGHER WALLS: ACTION, ACTIVISM AND EQUALITY IN THE BUILT ENVIRONMENT

1   Jonny Ball, '"Housing as a basic human right": The Vienna model of social housing', *The New Statesman*, 3 September 2019, www.newstatesman.com/spotlight/2019/09/housing-basic-human-right-vienna-model-social-housing [accessed May 2022].
2   'Quality of living city ranking (2019)', *Mercer*, https://mobilityexchange.mercer.com/Insights/quality-of-living-rankings [accessed May 2022].
3   '274,000 people in England are homeless, with thousands more likely to lose their homes', *Shelter*, 9 December 2021, https://england.shelter.org.uk/media/press_release/274000_people_in_england_are_homeless_with_thousands_more_likely_to_lose_their_homes.
4   *2020 Women's Budget Group Briefing: Housing and Gender*, 26 February 2020, https://wbg.org.uk/analysis/uk-policy-briefings/2019-wbg-briefing-housing-and-gender/.
5   John Harris, 'The end of council housing', *The Guardian*, 4 January 2016, www.theguardian.com/society/2016/jan/04/end-of-council-housing-bill-secure-tenancies-pay-to-stay.
6   'Full steam ahead at housing development on former Ebbw Vale Comp and college site', Blaenau Gwent County Borough Council, 2 August 2021, www.blaenau-gwent.gov.uk/en/news/full-steam-ahead-at-housing-development-on-former-ebbw-vale-comp-and-college-site/.
7   'Empty Properties', Blaenau Gwent County Borough Council, n.d., www.blaenau-gwent.gov.uk/en/resident/environmental-health/pollution/empty-properties/ [accessed May 2022].
8   'Dwelling stock estimates in England: 2021', Department for Levelling Up, Housing and Communities, 12 May 2022, www.gov.uk/government/statistics/dwelling-stock-estimates-in-england-2021.
9   David Cameron, 'David Cameron: I've put the bulldozing of sink estates at the heart of turnaround Britain', *The Sunday Times*, 10 January 2016, www.thetimes.co.uk/article/david-cameron-ive-put-the-bulldozing-of-sink-estates-at-the-heart-of-turnaround-britain-nk520rdrs.
10 Max L. Zarzycki, 'Filling in: Kiln Place in London, UK by Peter Barber Architects', *The Architectural Review*, 1 March 2021, www.architectural-review.com/buildings/housing/filling-in-kiln-place-in-london-uk-by-peter-barber-architects.
11 Jack Preece, 'To Demolish or Not to Demolish', *Greengauge*, n.d., https://ggbec.co.uk/embodied-carbon-and-building-demolition-the-case-for-retrofit/ [accessed June 2022].
12 Caroline Criado Perez, *Invisible Women: Exposing Data Bias in a World Designed for Men*, Chatto & Windus, London, 2019, p.30.
13 Criado Perez, *Invisible Women*, p.30.

9   FIELD: BIO-ARTS AS PLATFORM FOR COLLABORATION

1   FIELD has been showcased at the Lower Cavity artist-run residency programme (Massachusetts)

and exhibited at international venues including the Three Turns Miami Special Projects at the Untitled Art Fair in Miami, curated by artist Tony Labat; the CityXVenice Italian Virtual Pavilion, Biennale Architettura 2021, Venice, Italy, curated by Tom Kovac; and the 2021 Climate Provocations Pavilions on Governors Island in New York, curated by Ariane Harrison. FIELD has partnered with institutions including Columbia University, Pratt Institute and the University of Cincinnati. The project has been funded via several grants including the Franklin Furnace Fund for Performance Art (2021), the New York Foundation for the Arts City Artists Corps Grant (2021), the University of Cincinnati Faculty Award, and an 'On Our Radar' 2021 Creative Capital award. Workshops have been hosted by Guerilla Science, Barnard College, Columbia University, Pratt Institute, Wavepool Gallery and Civic Garden Center of Cincinnati.

2   Designed by Elizabeth Diller and Ricardo Scofidio, curated by Beatriz Colomina, Elizabeth Diller, Alessandra Ponte, Georges Teyssot, Mark Wigley, Richard Scofidio with Mark Wasiuta, *The American Lawn: Surface of Everyday Life*, Canadian Centre for Architecture, 16 June 1998 – 8 November 1999.

3   Marcus Fairs, 'Coronavirus offers "a blank page for a new beginning" says Li Edelkoort', *Dezeen*, 9 March 2020, www.dezeen.com/2020/03/09/li-edelkoort-coronavirus-reset/.

4   Mierle Laderman Ukeles's *Touch Sanitation* (1979–80) involved the artist travelling to all the boroughs of New York and personally shaking hands with every employee of the NYC Sanitation Department, saying the words 'thank you for keeping New York City alive'.

5   Part of the 'New Natural Resources and Emergent Labour Economies' project, which was supported by the Fulbright Visiting Scholar Fellowship at the Inclusive Ecologies Incubator, Pratt Institute.

6   Lydia Kallipoliti (ed.), *EcoRedux: Design Remedies for an Ailing Planet*, special issue of *Architectural Design*, vol.80, no.6, Chichester, John Wiley & Sons, November/December 2010.

7   Bruno Latour, *How to React to a Change in Cosmology*, Kyoto Prize Lecture, Cambridge, 2022.

10   ARCHITECTURE: ABOLISHED OR ABOLITIONIST?

1   Center for Sustainable Systems, University of Michigan, 2021, 'U.S. Material Use Factsheet', Pub. No.CSS05-18, September 2022, https://css.umich.edu/publications/factsheets/material-resources/us-material-use-factsheet. See also G.R. Matos, 'Materials Flow in the United States – A Global Context, 1900–2020', U.S. Geological Survey Data Report 1164, 2022, https://doi.org/10.3133/dr1164 [Supersedes USGS Fact Sheet 2017–3062].

2   See Lorie A. Wagner, *Materials in the Economy – Material Flows, Scarcity, and the Environment*, U.S. Geological Survey Circular 1221 (U.S. Department of the Interior and U.S. Geological Survey, 2022), https://pubs.usgs.gov/circ/2002/c1221/c1221-508.pdf.

3   See Keller Easterling, *Organization Space: Landscapes, Highways, and Houses in America*, MIT Press, Cambridge, MA, 2001, and *Extrastatecraft: The Power of Infrastructure Space*, Verso, London, 2014.

4   As the IPCC notes, 'Over the period 1990–2019, global CO2 emissions from buildings increased by 50%', Cabeza et al., 'Buildings', p.955.

5   United States Census Bureau, 'Highlights of 2021 Characteristics of New Housing', www.census.gov/construction/chars/highlights.html.

6   See Jacob Nchagmado Tagnan, Owusu Amponsah, Stephen Appiah Takyi, Gideon Abagna Azunre and Imoro Braimah, 'A view of urban sprawl through the lens of family nuclearisation', *Habitat International*, vol.123, no.102555, May 2022.

7   Graciela Fernández-de-Córdova, Paola Moschella and Ana María Fernández-Maldonado, 'Changes in Spatial Inequality and Residential Segregation in Metropolitan Lima', in Maarten van Ham, Tiit Tammaru, Rūta Ubarevičienė and Heleen Janssen (eds), *Urban Socio-Economic Segregation and Income Inequality*, The Urban Book Series, Springer, 2021.

8   Le Corbusier, *Vers une architecture*, Éditions G. Crès et Cie, Paris, 1925, p.xi.

9   Cabeza et al., 'Buildings', p.955.

10   See McKinsey Global Institute, *Reinventing Construction: A Route to Higher Productivity*, McKinsey & Company, New York, 2017.

11 Katherine McKittrick, *Demonic Grounds: Black Women and the Cartographies of Struggle*, University of Minnesota Press, Minneapolis, 2006, p.143.

12 'Since I Seen't You' was included on the album *Comin' From Where I'm From* which was released by So So Def Recordings and Arista Records in September 2003.

13 One hears the echo of *liberté, egalité, fraternité*. One hears the multilingual creole rhetoric of a democratic politics here, inflected with pan-African, anti-colonial, Caribbean histories of political thought.

14 For example, HOK's design for the $533 Million Wayne County Criminal Justice Center, a jail complex in Detroit. https://www.waynecounty.com/jail/home.aspx.

15 Such as activists, scholars and thinkers Angela Davis and Ruth W. Gilmore, among others.

11 HOME REVOLUTION: EQUALITY BEYOND REPRESENTATION IN THE WORK OF EDIT

1 The quote has been traced to novelist Rita Mae Brown's 1983 book *Sudden Death*, though according to other accounts it is even older than that. Andrew Robinson, 'Did Einstein really say that?', *Nature*, vol.557, no.7703, May 2018, p.30.

2 FAME Collective has been addressing some of these gaps through its research on ethnicity and gender.

3 Helen Hester, 'Material Hegemony Now: Domestic Realism and Financial Capitalism', in *A Section of Now: Social Norms and Rituals as Sites for Architectural Intervention*, Canadian Centre for Architecture and Spector Books, Leipzig, 2022, p.58.

4 Daniel Barber, 'After Comfort', *Log* 47, 2019.

5 Gloria Anzaldúa, *Borderlands/La Frontera: The New Mestiza*, Aunt Lute Books, San Francisco, 1987, p.109.

12 TOWARDS A QUEER ARCHITECTURAL HISTORY / UNTOWARD ARCHITECTURE

1 On the entanglement of class and sexuality in Britain, see Yvette Taylor, *Working-Class Queers: Time, Place and Politics*, Pluto Press, London, 2023.

2 Norman Potter, quoted in Robin Kinross, 'Herbert Read and Design', in David Goodway (ed.), *Herbert Read Reassessed*, Liverpool University Press, 1998, pp 145–62 (p.157).

3 Sutherland Lyall, 'A Passion for History and Architecture' [Review of John Harris, *No Voice from the Hall: Early Memories of a Country House Snooper*, John Murray, London, 1998], *Architects' Journal*, 7 May 1998.

4 Reyner Banham, 'Milan: The Polemical Skyline', *The Listener*, 1 September 1960, pp 338–40.

5 Samuel Medina, 'Is the Architecture Lobby the Bernie Sanders of Architecture?', *Metropolis*, 13 January 2017, https://metropolismag.com/profiles/architecture-lobby-bernie-sanders-architecture/.

6 Quoted in John Potvin, *Bachelors of a Different Sort: Queer Aesthetics, Material Culture and the Modern Interior in Britain*, Manchester University Press, 2021, which has both helped inform my understanding of the Labouchere Amendment and its importance, and strongly influenced the ideas and thrust of this essay.

BIBLIOGRAPHY

Action on Empty Homes, *Empty Homes in England 2020*, Action on Empty Homes, London, 2020

Antonelli, Paola (ed.), *Neri Oxman Material Ecology*, exh.cat., Museum of Modern Art, New York, 2020

Ardern, Jon, and Jain, Anab, 'More-Than-Human Manifesto', *Dezeen*, 18 November 2021, www.dezeen.com/2021/11/18/superflux-dezeen-15-manifesto-human-exceptionalism/

Assman, Jan, *Cultural Memory and Early Civilization: Writing, Remembrance, and Political Imagination*, Cambridge University Press, 2012

Barber, Daniel A., *Modern Architecture and Climate: Design before Air Conditioning*, Princeton University Press, 2020

Bennett, Jane, *Vibrant Matter: A Political Ecology of Things*, Duke University Press, Durham, NC, 2010

Bercsényi 28-30, Makovecz Imre, Budapest, 1981 M, http://bercsenyi2830.hu/node/80

Brown, James Benedict, Harriss, Harriet, Morrow, Ruth, and Soane, James (eds), *A Gendered Profession: The Question of Representation in Space Making*, RIBA Publishing, London, 2016

Calder, Barnabas, *Architecture: From Prehistory to Climate Emergency*, Penguin, London, 2021

Cheng, Irene, Davis, Charles L., and Wilson, Mabel O., *Race and Modern Architecture: A Critical History from the Enlightenment to the Present*, University of Pittsburgh Press, 2020

Choplin, Armelle, *Concrete City: Material Flows and Urbanization in West Africa*, John Wiley & Sons, New York, 2023

Colomina, Beatriz, 'Architectureproduction 1', in Kester Rattenbury (ed.), *This is Not Architecture: Media Constructions*, Routledge, London, 2002

Criado Perez, Caroline, *Invisible Women: Exposing Data Bias in a World Designed for Men*, Chatto & Windus, London, 2019

Easterling, Keller, *Extrastatecraft: The Power of Infrastructure Space*, Verso, London, 2016

Furman, Adam Nathaniel, and Mardell, Joshua, *Queer Spaces: An Atlas of LGBTQ+ Places and Stories*, RIBA Publishing, London, 2022

Hanley, Lynsey, *Estates: An Intimate History*, Granta Books, London, 2008

Hayden, Dolores, *The Grand Domestic Revolution: A History of Feminist Designs for American Homes, Neighborhoods, and Cities*, MIT Press, Cambridge, MA, 1982

Hopkins, Owen, 'Multiform and the Legacies of Post-Modernism', *Jencks Foundation*, 2022, www.jencksfoundation.org/explore/text/what-is-was-post-modern-multiform-and-the-legacies-of-post-modernism

Hopkins, Owen, and McKellar, Erin (eds), *Multiform: Architecture in an Age of Transition*, special issue of *Architectural Design*, vol.91, no.1, John Wiley & Sons, Chichester, 2021

Jain, Anab, 'Calling for a More-Than-Human Politics', *Medium*, 19 February 2020, https://medium.com/@anabjain/calling-for-a-more-than-human-politics-f558b57983e6

Jain, Anab, 'To doubt, to question, to say "enough"', *Civic Square*, 27 October 2022, https://medium.com/reimagining-economic-possibilities/to-doubt-to-question-to-say-enough-1f3334d774cb

Jain, Anab, 'Radical Design for a World in Crisis', *Noēma Magazine*, 25 April 2023, https://www.noemamag.com/radical-design-for-a-world-in-crisis/

Jencks, Charles, *Architecture 2000: Predictions and Methods*, Studio Vista, London, 1971

Jencks, Charles, *The Language of Post-Modern Architecture*, Academy Editions, London, 1977

Jencks, Charles, 'Death for Rebirth', in *Post-Modernism on Trial*, Architectural Design Profile, vol.88, Academy Editions, London, 1990

Kuhn, Thomas S., *The Structure of Scientific Revolutions*, University of Chicago Press, 1962

Le Corbusier, *Towards a New Architecture*, trans. Frederick Etchells (1931), Dover Publications Inc, New York, 1986

Le Corbusier, *Towards an Architecture*, translated by John Goodman with an introduction by Jean-Louis Cohen, Getty Publications, Los Angeles, 2007

Lichtenstein, Jacqueline, *The Eloquence of Color: Rhetoric and Painting in the French Classical Age*, University of California Press, Berkeley and Los Angeles, 1993

Matrix Feminist Design Co-Operative, *Making Space: Women and the Man-Made Environment*, Verso, London, 2022

Morrow, Ruth, Bridgens, Ben, and Mackenzie, Louise, *Bioprotopia: Designing the Built Environment with Living Organisms*, Birkhäuser, Basel, 2023

Moten, Fred, *The Universal Machine*, Duke University Press, Durham, NC, 2018

Parkin, Simon, 'Who Needs the Metaverse? Meet the People Still Living on Second Life', *The Guardian*, 10 June 2023, www.theguardian.com/technology/2023/jun/10/who-needs-the-metaverse-meet-the-people-still-living-on-second-life

Pollan, Michael, 'Why Mow? The Case Against Lawns', *The New York Times Magazine*, 28 May 1989, https://michaelpollan.com/articles-archive/why-mow-the-case-against-lawns/

Potvin, John, *Bachelors of a Different Sort: Queer Aesthetics, Material Culture and the Modern Interior in Britain*, Manchester University Press, 2015

Rajk, László, *Radikális Eklektika: Kölcsönzött Evidenciák*, Jelenkor Kiadó, Pécs, 2000

Richards, Marie-Louise, 'Pedagogies of Power: Education Within and Without the Institution', *The Architectural Review*, 1 September 2022, www.architectural-review.com/essays/keynote/pedagogies-of-power-education-within-and-without-the-institution

Savané, Vieux, and Diop, Baba (eds), *Matam: Construction en terre patrimoine intemporel*, Collège Universitaire d'Architecture de Dakar, 2019

Shelter, *Building for our Future: A Vision for Social Housing*, Shelter, 2019

Smith, Helen, *Masculinity, Class and Same-Sex Desire in Industrial England, 1895–1957*, Palgrave Macmillan, Basingstoke, 2015

Spencer, Douglas, *The Architecture of Neoliberalism: How Contemporary Architecture Became an Instrument of Control and Compliance*, Bloomsbury Publishing, London, 2016

Stephenson, Neal, *Snow Crash*, Bantam Books, New York, 1992

Sylla, Abdou, *L'architecture sénégalaise contemporaine: Sociétés africaines et diaspora*, Editions L'Harmattan, Paris, 2000

Tafuri, Manfredo, *Architecture and Utopia: Design and Capitalist Development*, MIT Press, Cambridge, MA, 1976

Taylor, Keeanga-Yamahtta, *Race for Profit: How Banks and the Real Estate Industry Undermined Black Homeownership*, University of North Carolina Press, Chapel Hill, 2019

Taylor, Yvette, *Working-Class Queers: Time, Place, Politics*, Pluto Press, London, 2023

The Architecture Foundation, 'The John Edwards Lecture 2010: Winy Maas and Philip Rosedale', 25 November 2010, www.vimeo.com/19083999

Urban Development Vienna, *Gender Mainstreaming in Urban Planning and Urban Development*, MA 18 – Urban Development and Planning, Vienna, 2013

Women's Budget Group, *2020 Women's Budget Group Briefing: Housing and Gender*, 26 February 2020, https://wbg.org.uk/analysis/uk-policy-briefings/2019-wbg-briefing-housing-and-gender/

Xiangning, Li, *Contemporary Architecture in China: Towards A Critical Pragmatism*, Images Publishing, Mulgrave, Victoria, 2018

INDEX

Note: *italic* page numbers indicate figures; page numbers followed by n. refer to notes.

AAP/ACE, 2023 (Jeyifous, 2023) *31*
abolitionism 142–5, 147–9
Action on Empty Homes (AEH) 113, 116
adaptation/reuse 63, 64, 83–4, 111, 113, 117–19
adobe *see* earthen constructions
American Lawn exhibition (Diller/Scofidio, 1999) 125, 169 n.2
architectural culture 17, 22, 25, 26, 29, 31–2, 35, 55
architectural discourse 13, 23, 24–5, 26, 29, 35, 53, 54, 97–101
architectural history 20, 21–2, *21*, *22*, 23, *24*
   see also queer architectural history
architectural media 13, 26, 29, 53, 54, 56, 97, 98
architectural style 13, 20, 21–2, 54, 144, 149
   and cycles 18–19, 22, 25
   pluralism in *see* pluralist architecture
   see also modernism; postmodernism
architecture
   as discipline 29, 32, 34
   and economics 18–19, 22, 23–4
   fragmentations of 26–8
   and hierarchy/patriarchy/elitism 18, 151–2, 155, 159, 161
   as profession 29, 33, 34
   and revolution 14, 37, 57, 141, 142, 143, 149
Archive of Affinities (Kovaks, begun 2010) *26–7*

ARM Architecture *12*
Arquia Festival (Barcelona, 2020) *86*, 90–93, *91*, *92*
artificial intelligence 63
Assemble 33, 34, 152
Asymmetrical Parallelism 51, 167 n.6

bacterial cellulose 109, *110*
bamboo 78, *78*, 109, *148*
Bamboo Theatre (Songyang County, Zhejiang, China) 78, *78*
Beechwood Mews (Barnet, London) 114, *115*
Belfast (UK) 35, *104*, *107*, *108*
Berman, Zoë 113, *120*
biomaterials 35, 42, 43–7, 77, 78, *78*
   bacteria/mycelium 109–11, *110*, 134, *140*, *141*
   earth bricks *see* earthen constructions
   grass-based *see under* FIELD
   typha (vegetal fibre) 47, 48, 49, 50
Black Box Research Group *140*, *141*
Braided Lives (Morane) *93*
Braiding FIELD (New York City Park, 2022) 131, *132*
Buckler, Charles Alban *158*, 159–60
building materials 19, 20–21, 25, 41, 50, 51, 100, 139
   sustainable *see* biomaterials
   see also concrete
building with 37, 145–9

Cameron, David 117
Capreesh, queer imaginary city of (Furman, 2022) *163*

carbon emissions/footprint 16, 21, 41, 47, 51, 94, 116, 119, 139–40, 141, 169 n.4
Casamance (Senegal) 42, *43*
China *see* Zhejiang province
class 99, 142, 152, 159, 161, *162*
climate crisis 16, 37, 59, 64, 71, 113, 142
Clip/Stamp/Fold exhibition (New York, 2006) 56
Cockerell, C.R. *21*
collaborative practices 35, 49–50, 105–11, 123, 127, 145
colonialism 16, 18, 21, *31*, 143
communication 50, 87, 89, 94, 95, 145, 146
Concentrico Festival (Logroño, Spain, 2021) *60*
concrete 19, 41, 50, *104*, 105–6, 107, *107*, 139, 141
COVID-19 pandemic 90, 93, 107, 114, 127
Crooke, Pat 159, *160*

Dakar (Senegal) 41, 43, *44*, *45*, 50, 51
decentralisation 26, 89, 127, 145
democracy/democratising approach 22, 50–51, 89, 146
Derrida, Jacques 32, 33
Diamniadio Lake City (Senegal) 41, *46*, 47
digital world 35, 54–6, 87–95, 105
Diller, Elizabeth 125, 169 n.2
DnA Design and Architecture 35, 77, 79–85
   and 'Architectural Acupuncture' 82–3, *83*

and industrial heritage 83–5,
   84, *85*
   Shangtian Village Transformation
      (2019) 80–82, *81*
   Shimen Bridge (2017) 79–80, *79*, *80*
Domestic Realism 152–3
Drone Aviary (Superflux, 2015) 63–4

earthen constructions 42, 43–4, *43*,
   44, *45*, 48, 49–50
ecology/ecosystems 35, 65, 68–70,
   71–3, 123, 131, 134
economics 18, 22, 23–4, 90
Edit 152–7
   Gross Domestic Product (2019)
      153, *153*, 155–7
   How We Live Now exhibition
      (2022) *155*, *156*, *157*
   Laundry Day (2021) *154*, 155, 157
Elementerre factory (Dakar,
   Senegal) 49–50
equity 113–21, 151–2
exhibitions 29–31, 33
*Exposition Internationale des
   arts décoratifs et industriels
   modernes* (1925) 17

Face, Pool, Two Towers and Ruin
   exhibition (Haszkovó Housing
   estate, 2019) *57*, 60
FIELD 35, 122–35, *122*, *124*, 168–9 n.1
   as attribute 124–5
   and awareness of nature 123–4,
      125, 129
   as concept 129
   as environment 129–31
   and grass-based biomaterials
      123, 125–9, *126–7*, *130*, *131*, *132*,
      133–4, *133*
   [moth] (2021) 127–9, *131*
   performance pieces of 131–2, *134*
Forensic Architecture 32–4, *32*
fragmentation, social/architectural
   26–8
Furman, Adam Nathaniel *58*,
   160–61, 162–6, *163*, *164*, *166*

Garden for Solitary Enjoyment, The
   (Qiu Ying, 1515–52) *76*, 78
gender *see* women
Gross Domestic Product (Edit, 2019)
   153, *153*, 155–7

Hamilton, Anthony 145–6
House from Grandma's Curtain (No
   Place House series, 2021) *52*
housing 21, 57–9, 142, 144, 153
   and carbon emissions 139–40
   crisis 113, 114
   equitable 113–21
   estates 14, 58, *112*, 117–19, *118*
   and labour/planning issues 100,
      100, *101*
   rural 80–82, *81*
   self-build 159
   virtual 94, *95*
How We Live Now exhibition (Edit,
   2022) *155*, *156*, *157*
human rights 22, 32, 113, 117
Hungarian architecture 53–4, *55*,
   59, *61*

industrial heritage 83–5, *84*, *85*
industrialisation 13, 14–16, 145
inequality/injustice 14, 16, 18, 21, 35–6
intellectual property 105–6
Invocation for Hope (Superflux,
   2021) 64, *66–7*, 68–70, *70*, 73

Jencks, Charles 20, 23, 24, *24*, 26, 56
Jeyifous, Olalekan *31*
Johnson, Philip 24–5
journals/magazines 13, 26, 29, 53,
   54, 56, 97

Keru Mbuubenne (Sendou, Senegal,
   2021) *40*, 44, 50
Kiln Place Estate (Camden, London)
   112, 117–19, *118*
Kinfrastructure *150*
Kovacs, Andrew *26–7*
Kővári, Györky *59*

Laboratory of the Future (Lokko,
   2023) 29
labour 77, 87, 99, *100*, 127, 132, 144,
   149, *150*
   household 152–3
land use/ownership 35, 109, 123, 131–2
laterite 43
Laundry Day (Edit, 2021) *154*, 155, 157
Le Corbusier 13–16, 37, 57, 58, 59,
   140–41, 142, 144, 145
   and architectural styles 13, 16, 19
   Villa Savoye (1928–31) *28*, *36*

Linden Homes (2010) 94
liquid modernity/architecture 35,
   89–90, 95
Lokko, Lesley 29
London (UK) *112*, 114, *115*, 117–19, *118*

MAK (Museum for Applied Arts,
   Vienna) *66–7*, 68
Matrix (feminist design co-
   operative) 152, *155*, *156*, *157*
metaverse 87–95
Mitigation of Shock (Superflux,
   2016) 64
Modern Architecture (Museum of
   Modern Art, 1932) 28, *29–31*
modernism 13–16, 22, 26–8, 31, 35,
   72, 141
   and digital world 54–5
   and inequality 14, 16, 18, 21
   and postmodernism 19, 20–21,
      23, 25
   and queer experience 162, 166
   as supercycle 19–20
modernity 13, 18, 21, 35, 41, 42, 89–90
'Modular Monkey' (Crooke, 1950)
   159, *160*
Modulor Man (Le Corbusier) *15*
Morane, Jenaia 93
More Than Human Manifesto, A
   (Superflux, 2021) *68*, *69*, *70*, 71–3
more-than-human perspectives
   35, 63, 64, *68*, *69*, 70, *70*, 71–3, *71*,
   105, 109
Museum of Modern Art (New York)
   28, 29, *143*
music 93, 145–6
mycelium 109, 134, *140*, *141*

New York (US) 56, 98, *99*, *100*, 127,
   131–2, 169 n.4
New York University (NYU) *96*, 98
Newcastle University (UK) 35, 107–11
NKD House (Worofila, 2021) 44, *44*,
   45, 47–8, *48*, 49, 50
No Place House series (2021) *52*

Oakland, California (US) 125
Overton window 23–4, 25, 29

Paradigma Adriané 54, *58*, 59–60
Part W 113, 119–21, *119*, *120*, *121*
passive design 48, *48*, 50, 51

patriarchy 37, 151, 155
Peter Barber Architects (PBA) *112*, 113, 114, *115*, 117, *118*
plastics 106–7, *108*
bio- *122*, 127–9
pluralist architecture 16–17, 19, 28, 31, 34, 59–60
Point Supreme *57*
pollution 16, 51, 139
polymers 106–7, *108*
postmodernism 19, 20–21, 23, 24–5, 31, 56, 56–7, 149
power 14, 21, 22, 153, 155
Presence of the Past, The (Venice Architectural Biennale, 1980) 29–31
Professor's Dream, The (Cockerell, 1848) *21*
Proud Little Pyramid (Furman, 2021) *166*
public parks 125, 129–31

Qiu Ying *76*, 78
queer architectural history 37, 159–66
and Buckler *158*, 159–60
and class 161, *162*
and criminalisation of homosexuality 165–6
and Crooke 159, *160*

R:R *138*, *143*, 147, *147*
race/racism 22, 89, *138*, 141, *143*, 170 n.13
and abolitionism 142–5, 147
and building with 37, 145–9
and slavery 37, 132, *144*, 147, 149
Refuge for Resurgence (Superflux, 2021) *62*, 64, *64*, 65–8, *65*, 70, 73
Republica (Robinson) *144*
reuse/adaptation 63, 64, 83–4, 111, 113, 117–19
Richards, Marie-Louise 18, 21
Rosedale, Philip 93, 94
rural architecture 35, *55*, 77, 78, *78*, 80–82

St Bartholomew Hut (Concentrico Festival, 2021) *60*
Scofidio, Ricardo 125, 169 n.2
Second Life (Linden Lab) 93–4, *94*, *95*

Senegal 41, 42
national architectural style of 51, 167 n.6
see also Worofila
Shimen Bridge (Songyang County, Zhejiang, China, 2017) 79–80, *79*, *80*
slavery 37, 132, *144*, 147, 149
social media 20, 54, *88*, 152
Songyang County (China) *see* Zhejiang province
Space Popular 90–93, *91*, *92*
Strada Novissima (Venice Architectural Biennale, 1980) *30*
supercycles 18, 19–20, 22, 24, 29
Superflux 35, 62–73
Drone Aviary (2015) 63–4
Invocation for Hope (2021) 64, 66–7, 68–70, *70*, 73
Mitigation of Shock (2016) 64
More Than Human Manifesto, A (2021) *68*, *69*, *70*, 71–3
and more-than-human perspectives 63, 64, 70
Refuge for Resurgence (2021) *62*, 64, 65–8, *65*, 70, 73
Supermrin 123, 125
supplement 32, 33
sustainable architecture 42–3, 47, 51, 116, 125
and rural communities 77, 82, 83–4, 85
see also biomaterials

Tactility Factory *104*, 105–6
technology 16, 18, 19, 63, 70, 72, 87, 89, 105–6
textiles *104*, 105–6, *107*, 148
Three Sons of John, 3rd Earl of Bute (Zoffany, c.1763–4) *162*
traditions, local 20, 21–2, 23, 34–5, 42, 49, 50
Transplastics project 106–7, *108*
12 Walls exhibition (2018) *58*, 60
typha (vegetal fibre) 47, 48, 49, 50

United States (USA) 18, 21, 125, 130, 134, 139, 140, 161
see also New York
universalism 16, 20, 22
urban planning/design 41, 72, 100, 113, 114, 116, 120, 123, 140, 141

urban sprawl 139, 140
urbanisation 35, 77, 85
urbanism 35, 88, 98

Venice Architectural Biennale 29–31, 30, *31*, *62*, 64
Vers une architecture (Corbusier) 13, 14, 140–41
Vienna (Austria) 113–14, 120
View of a Liberal Archive (Furman, 2020) *163*, *164*
Villa Savoye, Poissy, France (Le Corbusier, 1928–31) *28*, *36*
Virtual Guggenheim Museum (Asymptote Architecture, 1999) 90
virtual reality (VR) 87, 88, *88*, 89

Watkin, David 20
Wendling Estate (Camden, London) 117, *118*
women 106, 113, 119–21, *119*, 129, 132
in architectural practice 151–2
and transport systems 119–20, *120*
see also Edit
Worofila 34–5, 41–51
and biomaterials 42, 43–7
and collaborations 49–50
democratising approach of 50–51
Eco Pavilion, Diamniadio (2019) *46*, 47
Keru Mbuubenne (2021) *40*, 44, 50
NKD House (2021) *see* NKD House
and vernacular architecture 42–3, *43*

Zarzycki, Max L. 117
Zhejiang province (China) 77–85
'Architectural Acupuncture' in 82–3, *83*
Bamboo Theatre 78, *78*
housing project (2019) 80–82, *81*
industrial heritage in 83–5, *84*, *85*
Shimen Bridge (2017) 79–80, *79*, *80*
and sustainability 77, 82, 83–4, 85
Zoffany, Johan *162*

ACKNOWLEDGEMENTS

This is the Farrell Centre's first publication, so it offers an opportunity to acknowledge those who have been involved not just in the creation of this book but of the centre itself. Various Newcastle University colleagues past and present have been instrumental in the centre's development: Graham Farmer, Paola Gazzola, Nigel Harkness, Anya Hurlbert, John Pendlebury, Vee Pollock, Aerian Rogers, Julie Sanders, Adam Sharr and Terri Wishart. Luke Gardner of the university's estates team ran the building project, working closely with George Bamber and Ross Greenwell at Robertson Construction, and the architects, Chris Holmes and Ben Elliott. Lorna Burn, Abi Mitchell, Hannah Christy, Laura Chipchase Stuart, Hania Klepacka and our audience engagement team members have worked tirelessly in establishing the centre's programme and operations. But above all is Sir Terry Farrell, both for the generosity of his donation which made the whole endeavour possible and for the generosity of his vision for creating a place, where, to use his own words, 'people can come together to debate the city's future'.

The book originated in an online lecture series run in 2022/23, co-produced by the Farrell Centre and the university's School of Architecture, Planning and Landscape. We are hugely grateful to the contributors to that series (many of whom have also contributed to this book), to Mike West and Sarah Appleyard who helped deliver the series and to everyone who attended and asked questions that helped shape and refine the agendas explored in the present book. Many thanks to Val Rose at Lund Humphries for seeing the potential of turning the project into a book, Sarah Thorowgood for her patience, and Jacqui Cornish and Pam Bertram for shepherding it through production.

Finally, a very big thank you to the contributors to the book for their commitment to the project and the richness, originality and transformative energy of their essays. The book's overriding argument is for the enduring potential of architecture to reshape the world – a potential that can only be realised by a combination of ingenuity of vision and generosity of spirit, both of which are in abundance in the contributions to this book.

Owen Hopkins, Newcastle University